W9-CET-532

Guardian of Guadalcanal

The World War II Story of Coast Guard Medal of Honor Recipient Douglas Munro

Gary Williams

Published in the United States of America by The Lakota Press,
West Chester, OH 45069

Photographs used by permission of the U.S. Coast Guard and the
Munro/Sheehan families.

ISBN 978-0-9848351-4-0
eBook ISBN 978-0-9848351-5-7

Library of Congress Control No. 2013916402

Printed in the United States of America

For orders, please contact:

Bookmasters, Inc.
30 Amberwood Parkway
Ashland, OH 44805
Toll Free: (800) 537-6727
International: (419) 281-5100

Partial proceeds from the sale of this book benefit the:

Douglas Munro Scholarship Fund
c/o Coast Guard Foundation
394 Taugwonk Rd.
Stonington, CT 06378
(860) 565-0786

To GM2 Daniel Cannode, USCG, Vietnam, who first told me the story, and to Ray Evans, who lived it.

You never think about dying, even in that situation . . . You don't really think about it; you just do the job and you just anticipate that you're going to be OK, and then one day one of you isn't OK . . .

—Commander Ray Evans

CONTENTS

FOREWORD

"GUARDIAN OF GUADALCANAL"

The story of a young lad, Douglas Albert Munro, who actually was born in Vancouver, British Columbia, is as true of an American hero as many others who proudly served our country in time of war and selflessly gave his life protecting others. To suggest that this book is well overdue is an understatement. In my humble opinion, not only should a book have been written before this covering the life and heroic efforts of Signalman First Class Douglas Munro, but there also should have been a movie made—long ago, with iconic screen star John Wayne, or someone of his caliber, re-creating the events that made Munro the "Guardian of Guadalcanal." John Wayne? Yes, John Wayne! That's probably the best way I can explain just how far back I think a movie about Munro should have been made, not only for the sake of entertainment, but as a social media instrument during the post–World War II era, educating the public on one of America's best of the best!

Even though he was a young Coast Guardsman at the time of his death, Munro lived the life of a man who reflected the virtue of what is known today in the U.S. Coast Guard as its core values of Honor, Respect, and Devotion to Duty. Every Coast Guardsman, past and present, knows about Munro as a leader and a hero. Even more notably, the U.S. Marine Corps honors Munro as if he was one of their own, and says his name with pride, an emblem of their specific service core values of Honor, Courage, and Commitment.

Embracing the history, heritage, and traditions of the Coast Guard incorporated my own understanding of defining leadership. During my tenure as the eighth master chief petty officer of the Coast Guard, I had a full-size portrait of Munro hanging proudly in my office, right behind my desk. I wanted it there as my own personal reminder of how to perform my job as the service's senior-ranking enlisted member, charged with ensuring the health and well-being of every Coast Guardsman, especially making sure that enlisted members were represented in the day-to-day decision-making process managing the Coast Guard's workforce. There were days that I would just stare at Munro's portrait, and sometimes even have some quiet conversations with him, knowing that leadership through inspiration was a comforting and necessary thought process for me.

Recently, just after being asked to write the foreword to this book, I was in Seattle on a short, less-than-forty-eight-hour, business trip, which was quite a time challenge, given that I had flown from coast to coast. I didn't have much time to engage in very many nonbusiness social activities because of the compressed schedule. However, I just had to squeeze in about three and a half hours of driving time round-trip to head out to Cle Elum, Washington, to pay a visit to an old friend. It was that important to me to stop by the gravesite of Douglas Munro, and spend a few minutes carrying on those same spiritual conversations that I used to have when I was in my last active-duty assignment, before my retirement in 2002. This was my first visit to the Munro gravesite in more than twelve years. His legacy meant that much to me, so that this was one of, if not the most, important things that I had to do during that very short business trip.

I can only imagine how, after reading this book, your imagination may wander, bringing you to some understanding at least in part of what makes a hero. I love the story of Douglas Munro because it represents everything that defines the role of an inspiring leader, someone who, in the face of adversity and even death, seized the moment of despair, thinking not of himself, but of those five hundred Marines that he was responsible for, to ensure their safe passage, for the purpose of winning liberty and freedom for the oppressed.

Maybe you won't see things that deeply in your initial reading—but I can assure you from my years of telling the Munro story, ever since I learned of his heroic act that resulted in his posthumously being awarded the Congressional Medal of Honor, that his spirit of hope and compassion will follow you forever.

Vincent W. Patton III, Ed.D.
Master Chief Petty Officer of the Coast Guard (Ret.)

PREFACE

The United States Coast Guard is our oldest maritime service. Founded in 1790 by Secretary of the Treasury Alexander Hamilton as the Revenue Marine, by the 1860s the agency was generally referred to as the U.S. Revenue Cutter Service. The Coast Guard as we know it today was formed by the merger of five federal agencies—the Revenue Cutter Service, the Life-Saving Service, the Lighthouse Service, the Bureau of Marine Inspection and Navigation, and the U.S. Maritime Service, each of which had overlapping duties and authority.

The modern Coast Guard is a unique multimission military branch that operates under the Department of Homeland Security during peacetime and the Department of the Navy during times of war. It is unique because unlike other branches of the United States Armed Forces, which are prevented by federal statute and Department of Defense policy from acting in a law enforcement capacity, the Coast Guard is exempt from such restrictions. The Coast Guard has eleven distinct missions: ports, waterways, and coastal security; drug interdiction; aids to navigation; search and rescue;

living marine resources; marine safety; defense readiness; migrant interdiction; marine environmental protection; ice operations; and other law enforcement duties.

As one of the five branches of the military, the Coast Guard has been directly involved in every armed conflict from 1790 to Afghanistan. Because of its unique legal authority, the Coast Guard can conduct military operations under the Department of Defense or directly for the President. When not assigned to national defense, the Coast Guard carries out the duties and responsibilities of its other ten statutory missions.

After the war in Europe began in 1939, President Franklin D. Roosevelt ordered the Coast Guard to carry out what were called Neutrality Patrols to enforce the Neutrality Acts. The Neutrality Patrol was established in September 1939 as a U.S. response to the war in Europe. These patrols were responsible for tracking and reporting the movements of any hostile forces undertaking warlike operations in the waters of the Western Hemisphere.

In June 1940, the president gave the Coast Guard authority over "the anchorage and movement of all ships in U.S. waters and protected American ships, harbors and waters." As the war in Europe escalated, a federal law granted the Coast Guard jurisdiction over all ships that carried explosive ordnance and other dangerous cargo to protect U.S. ports and commerce.

In early April 1941, Greenland was added to the "hemispheric defense system." The Coast Guard was the only military branch equipped to operate in the unforgiving North Atlantic waters. With American involvement in the war imminent, President Roosevelt transferred the Coast Guard and all its resources to the Navy a month before the Japanese attack on the U.S. Pacific Fleet at Pearl Harbor.

During World War II, the Coast Guard manned 802 Coast Guard cutters. More than 49,000 Coast Guardsmen served on board 351 Navy ships, and nearly 7,000 Coast Guard personnel were deployed on 288 Army vessels. Coast Guard vessels sunk 11 enemy submarines, and landed Army and Marine forces in every invasion in North Africa, Italy, France, and the Pacific. Throughout the war, the Coast Guard had a total force of 171,000 enlisted personnel and officers, of which more than 80,000 served afloat. Nearly 2,000 Coast Guardsmen died, and an equal number were decorated: Six received the Navy Cross, one the Distinguished Service Cross, and one the Medal of Honor.[1]

Petty Officer First Class Douglas Albert Munro from South Cle Elum, Washington, was posthumously awarded the Medal of Honor by President Roosevelt "for extraordinary heroism and conspicuous gallantry in action above and beyond the call of duty" at Guadalcanal on September 27, 1942.[2] He remains the only member of the U.S. Coast Guard to receive the Medal of Honor. This is his story.

INTRODUCTION

Petty Officer First Class Douglas A. Munro, USCG, watched as the last of his boats return to Lunga Point Base near Point Cruz on the island of Guadalcanal. Manned by Munro's best friend, Coast Guard Petty Officer First Class Ray J. Evans, another Coastguardsman, and Petty Officer Second Class Samuel B. Roberts, USN, the boat was coming in full throttle. Evans was yelling and appeared to be waving at those ashore to clear the beach.

Tall and lanky and two weeks shy of his twenty-third birthday, Munro was the best small-boat operator on the island and leader of a squadron of twelve Higgins boats and six tank lighters.

The Landing Craft, Vehicle, Personnel (LCVP), more commonly called the Higgins boat, was a landing craft used extensively in amphibious operations during World War II. Designed by Andrew Higgins of Louisiana, the LCVP was based on boats built especially for use in swamps and marshes. Most commonly constructed of plywood, this shallow-draft, bargelike boat could transport a platoon-sized complement of thirty-six men to shore. Soldiers or Marines generally entered the boat by climbing down a cargo net hung from the side of a troop transport and exited by charging down the boat's bow ramp, which was lowered when the craft reached the shore.

The LCVP's companion boat, the fifty-foot ramped Landing Craft, Mechanized (LCM), commonly referred to by World War II veterans as tank lighter, was also developed by Andrew Higgins. This craft was used to land tanks, artillery, and other heavy vehicles during amphibious operations.

Munro's boat crews had just transported nearly six hundred men from the 1st Battalion, 7th Marines, under the command of Lewis "Chesty" Puller, then a lieutenant colonel, to a small cove just west of Point Cruz under intense covering fire from the USS *Monssen*, one of the destroyers off the island of Guadalcanal. Evans and Roberts had volunteered to remain behind to extract any wounded.

Roberts had been gravely wounded and the boat's throttle cable severed by enemy automatic-weapons fire when they steered the boat too close to the beach within range of Japanese gunners. Now Evans, unable to throttle back, hit the beach at about twenty knots, finally stopping about thirty feet onto the inclined shoreline. Munro ran toward the crippled boat as Evans yelled that Roberts had been hit. Munro jumped into the boat while corpsmen came running.

Evans knew that young Roberts's injuries were life-threatening. Both men stood back while the corpsmen frantically tended to the unconscious coxswain. Munro and Evans just looked at each other. When the litter arrived, Munro and Evans helped the corpsmen get Roberts off the boat and onto a waiting transport plane for evacuation to a nearby carrier, and from there hopefully to a hospital in Wellington, New Zealand.

With Roberts on his way to the carrier, Munro and Evans walked slowly up the long pier toward the operations building, neither man saying a word. Just before they reached the end of the pier, they noticed Commander Dwight H. Dexter, USCG, running toward them waving a piece of paper. He was obviously shouting, but neither Evans nor Munro could hear what he was saying over the deep throttling of the engines as the boats refueled.

Munro looked at Evans and said, "Whatever he's yelling about, it ain't good." Evans replied, "Never is." Doug smiled.

As Dexter reached the pair, he yelled, "Are you ready to go back and get those jarheads off that beach? They are getting hit pretty hard." Munro looked at Evans and said, "Hell, yeah!" Both men turned and ran back down the pier, yelling to the other boat crews to get ready to depart. They jumped into their boat, revved their engine, and prepared to shove off. With Munro and Evans in the lead, the squadron headed back out to sea.

After a few minutes, during which the boat crews could hear increasing enemy fire from ahead, the squadron approached the extraction point. Around them, enemy mortar fire caused violent percussive eruptions of water that towered above the flat-bottomed boats, drenched the crews, and decreased both maneuverability and visibility. Withering automatic-weapons fire from the beach splintered several of the plywood-hulled boats and whizzed past the heads of the crews. As the enemy fire increased, one of the boat crews pulled their craft alongside Munro's. They yelled that a rescue attempt was too dangerous and suggested they all return to Lunga Point Base. Munro responded by jabbing his finger toward the beach and yelled, 'We're not leavin' them there! We're goin' in!"

Still in the lead, Munro maneuvered his craft parallel with the shore while Evans provided covering fire from one of the boat's two World War I–era Springfield machine guns. Waves of haggard Marines ran from the beach into the water, dragging both the dead and the wounded, while more Marines poured onto the beach from the dense jungle. Clinging to the protected side of the boat, one wet, exhausted, and blood-covered Marine looked at Evans and said, "You came back, thank God, you came back." Evans pointed to Munro, who was maneuvering the boat. Evans directed the Marine to one of the boats behind them as waterspouts raised by Japanese automatic-weapons fire spiked across the water between the boats.

xviii GUARDIAN OF GUADALCANAL

Evans immediately looked back to check on the Marine, who gave him a thumbs-up and scrambled into the boat.

Within minutes, nearly five hundred vulnerable Marines had run into the water. Meanwhile, Japanese troops armed with mortars and automatic weapons had set up on the beach. Munro noticed that the men in the water were all but defenseless against the on-slaught of bullets and mortar fire and maneuvered his boat so that it was between them and the beach, giving the Marines cover. Once in position, Munro jumped into the other gun turret. He and Evans continued to provide covering fire while the last of the Marines loaded into the other boats.

With all boats apparently away, Munro turned the bow of his craft to begin the four-mile return trip to Lunga Point Base. It was then he saw that one of his boats was caught on a coral reef. Many of the Marines were back in the water, trying unsuccessfully to rock the boat loose. Munro maneuvered his craft alongside and called for a towrope to pull the boat loose. After several attempts, Munro's efforts were successful and the boat was freed. The exhausted Marines climbed back into the boat. During the rescue efforts, the Japanese had trained their mortars and automatic weapons on the boats, but both appeared to be out of range.

As Munro and Evans pulled their boat in behind the one they had just freed, Evans looked over his right shoulder and saw a trail of waterspouts coming across the water directly toward them. He yelled, "Doug, get down."

Doug didn't move or acknowledge Ray's warning.[1]

CHAPTER 1

WHY?

O n September 27, 2011, just before 0900, Commander
Douglas Sheehan, USCG (Ret.), and I turned off Douglas
Munro Boulevard and entered Laurel Hill Cemetery in Cle Elum,
Washington. Commander Sheehan's mother, Patricia, was Douglas
Munro's sister. The cemetery's meticulously kept landscape looked
like a marble garden surrounded by an emerald green carpet; the
towering ash, maple, and oak trees were just beginning their color-
ful autumn ritual.

We proceeded up the drive and looked to the right, where
two large gun mounts stood like sentinels before the tall nautical
flagpole with the flags fully extended in the brisk late-September
breeze. In the distance, a white concrete border appeared just above
the grass line topped with eight black posts linked by an anchor
chain. Inside the border, a single white military headstone stood
perfectly erect.

As we arrived and exited the car, the peaceful silence was broken only by the whispering sound of the wind as it passed through the towering pines that lined the driveway and the occasional banging of the lanyards against the flagpole. Through a fine mist, the gray overcast sky threatened rain. We were soon joined by Master Chief Petty Officer Jim Eidemiller, USN (Ret.), acting mayor of Cle Elum.

Two ladies from Cle Elum Florist arrived and placed two large ornamental red, white, and blue carnation wreaths on tripods, then set down a large, beautifully arranged floral arrangement near each of the five family headstones within the anchor chain border. After placing the floral arrangements, the ladies meticulously cleared each headstone of grass and debris, then stood silently for a moment.

By now, approximately ten members of the Douglas Munro Veterans of Foreign Wars Post 1373 had arrived and begun to set up chairs, a lectern, and a public address system on a nearby concrete pad. Several more cars now arrived. Exiting one of the cars was Sergeant Major Richard Smith, who led a platoon-sized contingent of Marines from Marine Corps Security Forces Battalion Bangor (the Marine Corps Security Forces are specialized units responsible for the security of naval installations). Dressed in their distinctive uniforms and white gloves, they assumed the setup duties from the aging veterans.

By 0930, the mist subsided; the area now saw a flurry of activity as the bugler, a firing party, veterans, media representatives, and Coast Guard personnel from nearby facilities arrived by the car- and vanload. Leading the Coast Guard contingent was Captain Lawrence Henderson, who served as the chief of staff for the 13th District, an administrative district based in Seattle that includes the states of Washington, Oregon, Idaho, and Montana. He was joined by Lieutenant Commander Jeffrey Pile; Master Chief Petty Officer of the Coast Guard Michael Leavitt, who held the highest rank for an enlisted person in the Coast Guard and reported directly to the commandant; Master Chief Petty Officer Jason Vanderhaden, command master chief for the 13th District; Master Chief Petty Officer William Lindsay; and about fifty other active-duty and reserve enlisted personnel.

As Command Master Chief Vanderhaden rose from his seat behind the lectern and approached the microphone to begin the ceremony, the clouds parted, the wind subsided, and a welcome ray of sunshine warmed those assembled. Following the pledge of allegiance and the playing of the national anthem, Master Chief Petty Officer of the Coast Guard Leavitt welcomed the large crowd, then rejoined the contingent of Coast Guard personnel standing behind the rows of chairs at parade rest. Command Master Chief Vanderhaden began reading Douglas Munro's Medal of Honor citation, and as the words "the President of the United States" echoed through the public address system the Marines and Coast Guard personnel snapped to attention. Veterans rose and stood silently throughout the reading of the citation. The rifle party fired a three-round volley, followed by the haunting notes of "Taps." At the conclusion, all uniformed military personnel resumed a parade-rest stance. After a moment of silence, Commander Sheehan delivered the keynote address.

> *On an average day in the Coast Guard, 12 lives are saved, 64 search and rescue cases are performed and a host of other actions are part of our day. Ours is a service with an abundance of heroes and role models. So why do we celebrate a single rescue that took place 69 years ago on September 27 every year? Usually, there are more than 50 people who drive for over an hour or more to a tiny cemetery in the landlocked community of Cle Elum, Washington for a ceremony to remember the story of Douglas Munro.*
>
> *The easy, obvious answer is that Douglas Munro is still, to this day, the only member of the U.S. Coast Guard who has ever been awarded the Medal of Honor. This is certainly special and unique.*

However, that is probably not the only reason. The fact that almost 500 Marines were saved that day is also a pretty big reason. That's not only a big number, but you also need to think about the wives, children and grandchildren of those 500 men. My mom died last December, and we had a gathering of friends and family at our house. One of my mom's very good friends said that if it hadn't been for her brother, she would not exist. Her dad was one of the Marines rescued in the evacuation in 1942.

In January, there was a ceremony on the Coast Guard Cutter Munro *in Kodiak, Alaska, to dedicate a bronze bust of my uncle, which is now part of their exhibit on the ship. One of the people at the ceremony was a woman from [Coast Guard] Station Kodiak whose grandfather had been rescued that day.*

Another special reason that we probably recognize this particular rescue is because my uncle was killed in action that day. Even though few Coast Guardsmen are killed in our rescue operations, it is almost always dangerous, and it is always a very real possibility that someone will die.

Something that is rarely mentioned about this event is that the highest honor ever awarded to any Coast Guardsman in the entire history of the service was awarded to an enlisted man: a first class petty officer. Our pay grade, rank and rate are an important part of our jobs, but at the end of the day, what is really important is, what did you really do today? I always smile whenever I read a front page newspaper story about a big rescue operation, and they quote a petty officer from the Coast Guard. I can't help but think that there is some Navy guy reading the article, and thinking, "Man, the Navy would never let a petty officer talk to the press!"

It continues to surprise me how often I am told by people outside of the Coast Guard, who say after hearing my uncle's story, "Gee, I didn't realize that the Coast Guard was involved in World War II." We have an ongoing battle with public perception about our military readiness missions. If you ask a Marine who was in one of those landing craft at Normandy, "Who would you rather have as your coxswain, a Navy or a Coast Guard guy?" I've heard some of them say that if they had a choice, they would prefer the guy with the most experience on small boats—the Coast Guard guy.

One of the common misconceptions of this event, like so many others, is that this is all about what happened in a few hours on a single day. The reality is that the action would not have been successful without a great deal of preparation. This part of what we do doesn't get much recognition or glory, but without it, we wouldn't be who we are. That is worth remembering on this September 27, and every other day.

In the Coast Guard, we tend to focus on what needs done, and this event underscores that. I think it is totally unfair that one person would live and the other would die, but that is just how things sometimes work out. I think this all speaks to a reality that we all accept in the Coast Guard.

Another important reason we remember today is because we realize that we need to pay some attention to Coast Guard history, just like our sister services. We need to take some time, once in a while, to recognize that if you don't remember where you have been, you can't really understand where you are going.

We wouldn't have a ceremony on September 27 if it hadn't been for Mike Cooley [Doug Munro's friend, who served in the Army in Europe]. He came home from World War II alive, and was sad that his boyhood friend did not. He raised and lowered the flag over my uncle's gravesite every day for 40 years. His actions inspired a lot of people in 1999 to install the light here at the gravesite, and to start an annual event. He was the leader of the Douglas Munro Veterans of Foreign Wars post in Cle Elum for many years. His VFW friends were at all the ceremonies: the burial after the war, my grandmother's funeral and at every September 27 ceremony we have had.

The next time you see a member of the VFW, thank them for their service and for their friend, Mike Cooley. He may not have been an official member of the Coast Guard, but his demonstration of Honor, Respect and Devotion to Duty makes him one of us. So, I think the real reason we get together every September 27, is because it reminds of why we do . . . what we do.[1]

Douglas Sheehan folded his notes and returned to his seat. Command Master Chief Vanderhaden thanked everyone for attending, then dismissed the crowd. Well over one hundred military personnel, veteran, family members, and patriots braved the chill and threat of rain to attend the memorial service for this highly decorated hero of Guadalcanal.

Of the more than 16 million Americans who served in World War II, only 464 were awarded the Medal of Honor, 266 of them posthumously. Names of heroes such as Lucian Adams, Eugene Fluckey, Matt Urban, and Audie Murphy were splashed all over American newspapers. The battle of Guadalcanal, a speck on the world map, resulted in twenty Medals of Honor. Lieutenant Commander Bruce McCandless, Major General Alexander Vandegrift, and Sergeant Mitchell Paige became household names.

However, before any of these heroes were recognized for their gallantry there was a twenty-two-year-old from the small town of Cle Elum in the middle of the Pacific Northwest, Petty Officer First Class Douglas Albert Munro of the U.S. Coast Guard.

So why do we celebrate a single rescue that took place more than seventy years ago on September 27 every year? This question naturally leads to several other questions: Who was Signalman First

Class Douglas A. Munro? What kind of man was he? Was the Coast Guard *really* involved in World War II? Did Munro *really* rescue five hundred Marines from the beaches of Guadalcanal? Did he *really* understand honor, respect, and devotion to duty? Did he *really* receive the Medal of Honor? Do the events of seventy years ago *really* affect the Coast Guard today?

CHAPTER 2

"MOTHER, ARE YOU OK?"

He was so excited, but you would never have known it by his demeanor. He spent most of his last evening in South Cle Elum with his best friend, Marion F. "Mike" Cooley.[1] The two had been nearly inseparable since early childhood.

Up before dawn, twenty-year-old Douglas Albert Munro packed and repacked his small suitcase. He had been getting ready for this day for the last month. Also awake and preparing for the day were his parents, James and Edith. James was extremely proud of the journey upon which his son was about to embark. His mother was less than excited about her baby leaving home. Doug's sister, Patricia, two years his senior, had left home and was attending secretarial school in Seattle.

EDITH "DEDE" THROWER-FAIREY Munro was born on April 16, 1895, in Egremomt, Wallasey, Liverpool, Lancashire, United Kingdom.[2] She was the eighth of twelve children born to William and Elizabeth "Lily" Thrower-Fairey. Just before the birth of his twelfth child, William was killed in an industrial accident in 1901 at the age of forty-three. Elizabeth decided to move her family to the Canadian province of British Columbia in 1910, to be close to her parents. She sent her oldest male children, Ernest and William, ahead. They settled in a large home on East King Edward Avenue in Vancouver, and then sent for the rest of the family. Edith, along with her mother and her remaining siblings, crossed the Atlantic on the SS *Tunisia*. After arriving in Nova Scotia, they traveled cross-country on the Trans-Canadian Railroad. Six days later, the family reunited in Vancouver.[3] Following her graduation from high school, Edith attended the Foncar Business College and graduated as a stenographer. While employed in Vancouver, she met James Munro.

James Munro was born James Wilkins on November 13, 1891, in Sacramento, California, to James and Elizabeth Wilkins. While James was a toddler, his parents divorced and his mother, along with James, emigrated to Canada in 1899. She subsequently met and married Daniel Albert Munro, who adopted James. An electrician by trade, James was employed at the Buntzen Lake Power Station near Vancouver when he met Edith. James and Edith were married in Vancouver's Christ Church, now the Christ Church Anglican Cathedral, on September 20, 1914. Immigration laws in effect at the time granted Edith naturalized American citizenship upon her marriage to James.[4] Soon after their marriage, James accepted a position with the Consolidated Mining and Smelting Corporation as chief operator of the company's electric power station in Trail, British Columbia. There, Edith gave birth to a daughter, Patricia Edith, on October 28, 1917, and a son, Douglas Albert, on October 11, 1919.

After Doug's birth, the Munro family moved to Vancouver, Washington, where James accepted a position as an electrician with the Warren Construction Company.[5] After James later took a job with the Chicago, Milwaukee, St. Paul & Pacific Railroad, the Munro family moved to the small remote town of Taunton, Washington. When the new substation in South Cle Elum, a small town located in Kittitas County in central Washington, was completed, James was tapped to be the operator.[6]

In South Cle Elum, the Munro family regularly attended the local Episcopal Church, where both Patricia and Douglas were baptized. James became active in local veteran's affairs and organizations and served as a captain in the Washington State Guard Reserve. Edith was a member of social organizations and church-related groups, but spent the bulk of her time caring for her children.[7]

As DOUG AND his father talked intently in another room, Edith sat at her small kitchen table. Her thoughts began to wander. The youngster who had spent hours at the Milwaukee Road depot working with his father had grown into a young man and was now leaving home.[8]

The world in which they lived was changing quickly, and not for the better. The year was 1939, and America was engulfed in the Great Depression. Overseas, war in Europe seemed inevitable, and the threat of global conflict worsened with each passing day. Nevertheless, life for the Munro family remained comfortably routine. James was an active member of the local American Legion Post, which sponsored the local Sons of the American Legion drum and bugle corps, for whom he served as director. Doug was an enthusiastic member of the corps, which was made up of about twenty drummers and thirty buglers. During Memorial and Veteran's Day ceremonies, Doug was called on to honor local veterans by playing "Taps."[9]

Munro family vacations frequently consisted of trips to Washington's Pacific coast forests and beaches. Doug climbed up on huge rocks that lined the beach to look out across the water. Under the watchful eye of his father, Doug used a wooden plank to paddle out into the churning surf and ride the waves into shore. Patricia was content to play in the beach sand with her mother.[10]

While Doug, known as "Buddy," had many friends, he was closest to Mike Cooley, Dale Cox, and Dean Gordanier. He and his friends spent a lot of time at the substation and train depot. They quickly learned that a smile would get them cookies and other treats from the waitresses at the depot's restaurant and rides atop stacks of luggage by the baggage handlers.[11]

Gifted in music, Doug mastered the drum, the bugle, and the harmonica, and played the trumpet in the Pep Band, the Senior Orchestra, and the Dance Orchestra in high school. Unbeknownst to his parents, he had also become an exceptional dancer. He became the march leader and music director for the corps, whose practices and close-order drills were conducted on a vacant lot next to the Munro home. All of the hours of practice paid off when the Sons of the American Legion won the American Legion Junior National Championship in 1934. Doug was also a gifted and natural athlete, participating in wrestling, tumbling, and basketball. He was a member of the 1934 high school state champion basketball team. He joined Boy Scout Troop 84 in Cle Elum and attained the rank of Life, just below that of Eagle Scout.[12]

Growing up, Doug and his sister walked the four-mile round-trip to and from school every day and were extremely close. Oftentimes they took to the slopes for hours of skiing in the winter and long hikes and overnight camping trips during the spring and fall. They spent many evenings on the family front porch swing or on long walks in conversation. When Patricia left home to pursue her secretarial studies in Seattle, both missed their talks.[13]

Following graduation from high school in June 1937, Doug enrolled at Central Washington College of Education, now Central Washington University, in nearby Ellensburg, which allowed him to continue to lead the Sons of the American Legion. While attending Central Washington, he lived at home, commuting to school each day. Doug studied business and became the "Yell King" at sporting events. He learned quickly that there was a whole new world outside of Cle Elum. Although he was an excellent and outgoing student, during his sophomore year he quickly began to lose his enthusiasm for his studies. Doug frequently commented to his parents how socially and politically isolated he was in Cle Elum, wondering aloud what lay beyond the Cascades and the other side of the Pacific—much to the astonishment of his mother, but much less so his father. Edith had not previously recognized Doug's interest in geopolitical affairs.[14]

Once, during a passionate dinner conversation, Doug told his parents that nationwide, one-quarter of the workforce was out of work. In the Pacific Northwest, where the major industries were mining and logging, unemployment far exceeded the national average, and entire industries were all but destroyed. Tent cities had popped up throughout the region as families lost both their jobs and homes. Families had been reduced to scavenging for food on the streets and standing in line at the few available soup kitchens. Living through the Great Depression, James and Edith were all too aware of how severe the national and regional economic climate had become and were surprised by Doug's apparent understanding of the economic plight of the country.[15]

Although the Munro family had been spared the economic hardship that befell many in their hometown, Doug felt empathy for those who lived on the streets and came to the church to pick up food. Using a wheelbarrow, he and Mike Cooley earned money by delivering orders for coal for a local vendor to those who could afford it, and gathered and split wood from surrounding forests and delivered it to those who could not. He was frustrated by the economic hardships of those who eagerly and actively sought work but could find no jobs. His eyes had been opened, and from the passion with which he talked, Edith knew that Doug had set a course dedicated to helping others.[16] Helping others, that certainly described Doug.

She also remembered sitting with Doug and her husband listening to President Roosevelt's radio addresses, known as fireside chats. As a result of his college classes and interaction with classmates, Doug's interest in social and political affairs had increased, and he would ask numerous questions following the president's remarks. Her son had grown up so quickly. Too quickly? she wondered.[17]

On the other side of the globe, Germany was under the dictatorship of Chancellor Adolf Hitler and his Nazi Party. Although the Treaty of Versailles, which had ended World War I, imposed strict disarmament terms on Germany, Hitler had dropped all pretenses of adherence to it and began rapidly rebuilding the country's military. A year earlier Germany had "annexed" Austria. Despite the growing threat of German expansionism, the governments of both Britain and France adhered to a policy of appeasement toward Hitler.

Hitler demanded that Czechoslovakia cede to Germany a territory along the German-Czech border. At the 1938 Munich Conference, British prime minister Neville Chamberlain and French prime minister Édouard Daladier accepted Hitler's demand contingent upon his agreement to forgo any further territorial seizures. Most likely reassured by British and French inaction, Hitler ignored the terms he had agreed to and threatened to invade other neighboring countries. As a result, world tensions were rising.

In early September 1939, Hitler made good on his threat and invaded Poland. While the United Kingdom and France demanded immediate German withdrawal, the British army mobilized in preparation of anticipated German air attacks. The Chain Home system, a ring of coastal early warning radar towers, had been constructed the previous year, and now operated around the clock. World governments reacted frantically to the German invasion, and within two days the United Kingdom, Australia, New Zealand, and France declared war against Germany.

Edith recalled that one evening at dinner Doug had told them about the talk on campus about possible compulsory enrollment for military service, which brought a momentary silence to the conversation. Doug said that he could enlist or wait to be drafted. Edith had dropped her fork onto her plate, which startled everyone, and the topic of conversation was quickly changed.[18]

While officially the United States maintained a posture of neutrality, Doug told his parents that he believed that it was just a matter of time before the country entered the war. Certainly the United States would not stand by idly and allow German domination of England. The thought was unspeakable.

Doug spent several weeks researching each branch of the service. Having made frequent trips to the Washington coastline with his family, he had set his mind on one of the sea services. He quickly eliminated the Marine Corps, which left the Navy or the Coast Guard. He had spent several days talking with his father as well as veterans at the American Legion post about the different branches of the military. Unbeknownst to his parents, he had made at least one trip to the Navy recruiting office and several trips to the Coast Guard recruiting office, both in Seattle. He ultimately decided that the multimission Coast Guard gave him the greatest opportunity to help others as well as the chance to travel. After he reached the decision to enlist, he immediately informed his sister, who promised not to tell anyone until Doug had broken the news to his parents. Patricia remembered Doug telling her "the Coast Guard is focused on saving lives, not taking them."[19]

After Doug signed his enlistment papers, he failed his preenlistment physical examination for being underweight. On his way home, he stopped by his father's office and talked to him about his enlistment. After he told his father that he needed to put on six pounds in the next ten days, James chuckled and said, "Your mother certainly can take care of that." Then Doug and his father walked home.[20]

Edith winced as she recalled the day when Doug informed her that he had dropped out of college and had enlisted in the Coast Guard, but managed a slight smile as she recalled when he told her of his need to put on weight before his enlistment date, which was two weeks away. She knew that she could fatten him up in time for his next enlistment physical examination. Edith knew Doug was restless and had tired of small-town life. Whatever plan God had for her son, it was not in Cle Elum.[21]

As both men entered the kitchen, Doug inquired, "Mother, are you OK?"

Edith snapped back to the present as the two most important men in her life looked at her with concern. She nodded affirmatively and slowly got up from her chair.

"It's time to go," James said softly.

As Doug and his father walked out to the car, Edith slowly gathered her purse and jacket. Before leaving, she entered Doug's room, glanced around, and wondered aloud when he would return. On her way to the car, she walked back through the kitchen and softly caressed Doug's chair.

"Edith?"

She quickly looked up and saw James standing in the doorway. The expression on her face spoke volumes. He walked over and gave her a gentle hug. She took a deep breath and gathered herself. Together, Edith and James turned and walked hand in hand out to the car. It was, indeed, time to go.[22]

His parents planned to drive him the ninety miles to the Seattle Federal Building and the Coast Guard Recruitment Office. Apparently wanting to spare both himself and his parents an emotional good-bye, Doug jumped out of the car while it was stopped at a downtown intersection, grabbed his small suitcase, tipped his hat, and said, "So long, folks." He looked at his mother and said, "Don't worry." Although slightly shocked, she smiled. Doug and his father made eye contact for several seconds; both just nodded. No words were necessary. They already said what needed to be said. As he reached the sidewalk, he heard his mother cry out, "Douglas!" He turned, smiled, and again tipped his hat.[23]

After parents drove away, he began walking. He soon approached the large concrete steps leading up to the front door of the Federal Building, where he met another young man carrying a suitcase. As they reached the door, the other man said, "Looks like we're headed to the same place. Hi, I'm Ray Evans."[24]

With a big smile, Doug replied, "It sure looks that way. I'm Doug Munro."[25]

The two young men had arrived at the recruitment office under entirely different circumstances. Doug had enlisted for the chance to help others and travel. That was not the case for Ray.

Raymond J. Evans Jr. was born February 2, 1921, in Bellingham, Washington. His father worked the Long Lines Division of the Pacific Telephone & Telegraph and the family relocated frequently. Ray and his family settled in Cle Elum in 1925 when his father supervised the local telephone office however, Doug and Ray never met. When Ray's father was transferred back to Bellingham in 1934, Ray moved to Blaine and spent the next four years living with friends on a large family farm.[26] Located in the northwest corner of the state, Blaine lies near the U.S.-Canadian border.

Entering Blaine High School in 1936, Ray was an excellent student and participated in boxing, football and basketball. Ray's participation in boxing was short-lived when he learned that his jaw could not take the direct blows. In 1938, Ray returned home to his family, now living in Seattle for his junior year at Broadway High School, where he continued his participation in football and basketball until his graduation in 1939.[27]

Ray remembered, "My dad read the dictionary three times from cover to cover. He taught himself three new words every week, and used them so that he would remember how to use them and what part of speech they were". Ray later said that he used the same technique for the next fifty years.[28]

After graduation, he had looked without success for permanent work, taking odd jobs to survive. He had previously attempted to enlist, but was told that the Coast Guard had not taken a recruit in nearly seven years, due to a downsizing in personnel following World War I. A few days before meeting Doug, the Coast Guard called Ray and asked if he was still interested in signing up. Ray asked about the sudden change and received the reply, "We have seven openings; do you want one or not?" Ray accepted. Although he only had a few days to prepare, Ray recalled, "It didn't matter because I wasn't married and I didn't own anything except the few clothes I packed in the suitcase someone gave me."[29] What Doug and Ray did not know was that seven days earlier, President Roosevelt had authorized the Coast Guard to add two thousand men to its ranks.

The first order of business was a physical examination. Doug was measured at five feet eight and a half inches tall and weighed in at 138 pounds, the absolute minimum weight for his height. Hearing the news, Doug just smiled. Seeing his smile, Ray said, "What's that for?" Doug replied, "I actually had to put on weight to get this job. Can you believe that?" Patting his stomach, Ray replied, "I sure don't have that problem." Both laughed.[30]

After reciting their oath of enlistment, Douglas Munro and Ray Evans joined ten other enlistees, known as seamen apprentices, in completing the required paperwork. Doug, Ray, and the other new recruits were told that while a boot camp was being constructed at the Old Quarantine Station in nearby Port Townsend, it had not yet been completed, and they would be bused to Air Station Port Angeles for their training.[31]

The officer in charge handed Ray twelve one-way bus tickets, one for each of the new recruits, and informed the group that Ray was in charge until they reached their destination. Ray recalled, "Why he handed me those tickets and put me in charge is beyond me, probably because I was standing closest to him at the time." When the bus arrived, Ray handed each man a ticket, and counted them as they boarded. He was the last to climb aboard for the two-hour trip.[32]

Other than the driver, the Coast Guard's newest recruits were the only passengers on the bus. During the ride to their destination, Doug and Ray talked and got to know each other as well as some of their fellow recruits. While a few boasted about their potential for promotion, most sat quietly staring out the window.[33]

Chosen for its strategic location in the defense of the Northwest, Air Station Port Angeles had been established four years earlier as the first Coast Guard air station on the Pacific Coast. When the new recruits arrived at the facility, the staff there was at a loss as to what to do with them. Because the Coast Guard had not taken any new recruits for a number of years, training programs had long been disbanded. According to Ray, "they didn't know what to do with us, so they had us peeling potatoes, performing simple maintenance on the boats, and mowing grass; the usual things you see in the cartoons. That was our training back then."[34]

On the third day, during morning announcements, the new men learned that the Coast Guard cutter *Spencer* was being permanently reassigned from Alaska to New York and was in need of seven recruits to fill out its crew. Doug and Ray wasted no time in getting over to the administration building to sign up, but they were not the only ones with the same idea. A line had already formed; when they joined it, Doug was seventh and Ray eighth. Doug was selected, but Ray would have to wait until the ship arrived to learn his status.[35]

That evening, Doug telephoned his parents and sister to let them know of his departure. James and Edith were unable to make it down on such short notice, but Patricia took the day off from her studies and drove to Port Angeles to see him off. As fate would have it, when the *Spencer* arrived, one of the selected recruits withdrew his request and Ray replaced him.

At the time, young Douglas Munro could not have imagined how historically important his enlistment would become, and neither he nor Ray could have realized the magnitude of that day. Hundreds of men would live, and thousands would have the opportunity at life, as a result of their choice, friendship, and selfless actions, a legacy and posterity that circles the globe and continues nearly seventy years later. Historians and military authors later wrote that their joint enlistment created one of the most significant relationships in American military history.

CHAPTER 3

THE NORTH ATLANTIC

The Coast Guard cutter *Spencer* arrived at Port Angeles in the early morning hours of September 21, 1939. Doug and Ray had been packed and ready to board since dawn.[1] The *Spencer* was one of the seven "Treasury" or "Secretary" class cutters named for former secretaries of the Treasury Department. Commissioned two years earlier, the *Spencer's* namesake was John C. Spencer, a veteran of the War of 1812 who served in the House of Representatives from 1817 to 1819. He had been appointed by President John Tyler as secretary of war in 1841, and subsequently became the sixteenth secretary of the treasury in 1843.[2]

Built at the Brooklyn Navy Yard based on the *Erie*-class gunboat design, the *Spencer's* propulsion system consisted of two Westinghouse double-reduction geared turbines supplied with steam from oil-fired boilers that drove twin exposed screws. With a

41-foot beam, the steel-hulled 327-foot cutter was capable of just over twenty knots, and had an authorized crew complement of 16 officers and 107 enlisted. Its only armament was two five-inch guns, but it carried a Grumman J2F Duck, a single-engine amphibious biplane used primarily for utility and air-sea rescue duty.[3]

Based in Dutch Harbor, Alaska, the *Spencer* was assigned to the Bering Sea Patrol. In addition to performing special transport missions, the ship enforced maritime regulations, conducted search-and-rescue operations, and maintained aids to navigation for Alaska's all–important fishing industry. On September 2, 1939, having arrived back at its homeport after a ninety-day deployment, the crew was put on leave, except for those men needed for maintenance and watch rotations.[4]

The following day, all Coast Guard ships received a dispatch reporting that a state of war existed between England and its ally, France, and Germany, and advising all ship commanders to judge their actions accordingly. On September 5, 1939, President Roosevelt declared that the use of U.S. territorial waters for hostile actions would be regarded as unfriendly, offensive, and a violation of official U.S. neutrality. That same day, all leave was canceled, and the crew was ordered back to the ship. There they were informed that the *Spencer*, along with the cutters *Duane*, *Alexander Hamilton*, and *Ingham*, had been transferred to the jurisdiction of the Navy and were to be permanently deployed to the East Coast. The *Spencer* was headed for Staten Island, New York. No other details were given. After the announcement, crew members rushed or called home to inform their families of the news, leaving their wives to sell homes or break lease and rental agreements and make their way across the country, many with small children.[5]

The *Spencer* took on five hundred tons of fuel oil and additional food and maintenance supplies, and weighed anchor within forty-eight hours. Routine and restorative maintenance would be completed at sea. Several crew members short, the ship was directed to Port Angeles to fill its crew complement.[6]

Though Port Angeles provided a natural deep-water channel more than capable of handling the ship's draft, to save valuable time, the *Spencer* dropped anchor well offshore. Doug, Ray, and the other new crew members ferried out to the ship to report for duty.[7] After the last man stepped on board, the *Spencer* again weighed anchor and began its 5,400-mile voyage to New York.

In response to the increasing drumbeat of war in Europe, on September 8, President Roosevelt declared a limited national emergency and authorized a call-up of reserves. Most Americans noticed no change in their daily routine, but not members of the military.

A month earlier, at the request of British prime minister Winston Churchill, President Roosevelt had provided England with twelve merchant freighters loaded with a wide assortment of arms that included bombers, tanks, rifles, machine guns, Browning automatic rifles, and 100 million rounds of ammunition to demonstrate his support of Great Britain. Despite the assistance, Great Britain was in great danger of being overrun by Germany. Again in response to an urgent request from Churchill, and without congressional approval, Roosevelt gave the British fifty surplus destroyers in a ships-for-bases agreement that resulted in the United States obtaining the rights to use British airstrips in the Atlantic region.[8]

On board the *Spencer*, Doug and Ray were assigned as quartermasters and found themselves in a whole different world of unique terms, slang, customs, and skills. Their fellow recruits who volunteered for engineering duties were assigned to the Black Gang. As new quartermasters, Doug and Ray were assigned to Deck Force, responsible for maintaining all of the rescue and survival equipment, initiating all navigational publications and directives, and maintaining all deck equipment and the overall appearance of the ship's exterior. They had the additional responsibilities of monitoring navigational instruments and clocks and the instruction of the ship's lookouts and helmsmen.[9] The training was rigorous and thorough; it had to be at sea, where there is no room for error.

Long days and short nights were soon the normal schedule. Even the most routine tasks, such as walking, became a skill to be mastered. With new skills, routines, and shipboard culture to learn, the days passed quickly. At sea, everything ran on a tight schedule—everything. Doug had enlisted in the Coast Guard for the opportunity to travel and to help others. He did both. Each man was dependent on all of his shipmates to do their jobs correctly, on time, every time.

As best friends, Doug and Ray were always together, and though they did not look alike, many of the crew got them confused—so much so that it became a running joke. One of the crew had referred to Doug and Ray as the "Gold Dust Twins." Gold Dust was a popular soap compound distributed by Lever Brothers at the time. The product was easily recognized by its bright orange label, on which the figures of twins called Goldie and Dustie were humorously depicted. The original Gold Dust Twins were the faces of the product line. The nickname stuck immediately, and for the duration of their time on board, Doug Munro and Ray Evans were known as the Gold Dust Twins.[10]

As the *Spencer* entered the Gatun Locks of the Panama Canal, it received orders to join a Navy task force to search for the German heavy cruiser *Admiral Graf Spee,* which had been wreaking havoc on Allied merchant shipping in the South Atlantic. Military officials believed that the German warship had violated U.S. neutrality and entered U.S. territorial waters. After several days of an unsuccessful search, the *Spencer* was ordered to resume its course for New York. Ray later recalled, "That German cruiser was heavily armed. We only had two five-inch guns. I don't know what we would have done if we had found it."[11]

While work consumed the overwhelming majority of the crew's time and energy, some recreation time was available. Wrestling matches were a favorite stress-relieving activity for the crew. Using the name "Bunting Tosser Munro," Doug dusted off his high school wrestling skills and participated in several matches in a makeshift ring on the ship's stern. His record was not all that impressive, Ray recalled, but "Doug sure had a good time. I enjoyed watching him."[12] Doug earned the respect of his shipmates because he was not afraid to take on guys much larger than him and always gave them all they could handle. While his technique wasn't all that good, he was very quick, which made him hard to catch and even harder to hang onto; his long arms and legs gave him reach and step advantage. His tenacity earned him even greater respect.[13]

The *Spencer* dropped anchor at New York's Pier 18 amid a mid-November snowstorm. For the Gold Dust Twins, it came at a perfect time. The New York World's Fair had opened earlier in the year and was in full swing. Reared in a small city, Doug and Ray had never seen anything like it. The fair, which had opened with the stated purpose of lifting the spirits of the Great Depression–ridden United States and to bring much-needed business to New York City, saw more than two hundred thousand visitors daily. Doug and Ray joined the throng at every opportunity.[14]

As the *Spencer* was being readied for its new role, Doug and Ray noticed a sense of urgency that was palpable. According to Ray, "Everybody was given more than one job to do. That's just the way it was. There was no complaining. We all had multiple jobs to do and we did them."[15] The work was long, hard, and intense. Everyone suspected what lie ahead, but no one spoke of it openly. Privately, however, everyone on board believed that the armament overhaul, coupled with the deteriorating conditions in Europe and the report of the German sinking of thirty-seven Allied cargo vessels in the North Atlantic over the previous days, signaled that war was imminent.[16]

A couple of weeks after their arrival in New York, a cough and fever that Doug had dismissed as a chest cold rapidly worsened over the course of a few hours. By the time Ray was able to get him to sick bay, Doug was incoherent. Ray was very concerned about his friend. Doug was immediately transferred to the Staten Island

Naval Hospital, where doctors diagnosed him with a severe case of pneumonia in both lungs. He spent more than a week in the hospital, and after his discharge, he was put on limited duty for another couple of weeks. Ray recalled that it was an additional two weeks before Doug regained his color and was back to his "normal self."[17]

Back in Seattle, Patricia was working in a law firm as a legal secretary when she met John Burton "Burt" Sheehan, a young paint chemist who was seeking advice about starting his own company. Pat sent Doug a lengthy letter telling him all about "Burt" and getting Doug caught up on the news in Cle Elum.[18]

ROOSEVELT WAS REELECTED to a third term in a landslide in November 1940. On December 3, he boarded the USS *Tuscaloosa*, a *New Orleans*–class heavy cruiser, under the pretext of taking a vacation in the Caribbean. While he was on board, the president's visitors included a steady flow of British dignitaries. Now sixteen months into the war with Germany, Great Britain could no longer pay for its military weapons and supplies; however, abandoning the English was not an option. Creative problem solving was needed. At the end of his vacation, Roosevelt announced his intent to initiate the Lend-Lease program, which would provide American arms to the British in exchange for in-kind (i.e., ships, canned rations, motor vehicles, telephone cable, and clothing) repayment after the war.

With the horrors of World War I still fresh in Americans' minds, Congress had passed legislation in 1935, 1936, 1937, and again in 1939, all designed to maintain U.S. neutrality in the event of another European conflict. Despite the German invasions of its European neighbors, powerful forces in Congress pushed for non-interventionism and strong Neutrality Act compliance. Although privately President Roosevelt strongly opposed U.S. neutrality in the war in Europe, his public position was in accord with official American policy. However, Hitler interpreted the proposed Lend-Lease program as an act of aggression against Germany.[19]

In response to Hitler's stance, Roosevelt addressed the approached the Governing Board of the thirty-five member Pan American Union on May 27, 1941, to initiate and organize a Neutrality Patrol in both the Atlantic and Pacific Oceans. Although the Neutrality Patrol was a Pan American initiative, no nation other than the United States was able to provide the ships capable of carrying out such an endeavor.

The stated objective was to track and report on any Axis Power's air, surface, or underwater naval forces that approached the United States or the West Indies, but the real purpose was to demonstrate to the world the readiness of the U.S. Navy to defend the Western Hemisphere. During the planning stage in Washington, two critical limitations were quickly detected. First, the Navy did not have the number of ships needed to properly conduct such a global initiative; second, Navy destroyers were ill-suited for duty in the treacherous waters of the North Atlantic. In preparation for the neutrality patrol, Navy officials, in consultation with the Coast Guard, received presidential authorization in the spring of 1941 to transfer six of the Coast Guard's Secretary-class cutters to service with the Navy.[20]

With their hull form, wide beam, ample power, heavy displacement, and a range of eleven thousand nautical miles, the *Spencer* and its sister ships proved to be well suited for the outer limits of the patrol. To compensate for both of the Navy's limitations, planners decided that the Navy would be responsible for the warm waters of the Pacific and the Coast Guard the unforgiving Atlantic.

The *Spencer* was assigned to the newly created Neutrality Patrol. When the commander of the Boston District assumed control of the Neutrality Patrol, he renamed them the Grand Banks Neutrality Patrols.[21] The patrol cruised in a continuous pattern two hundred miles off the coast of Newfoundland's Grand Banks, then south through the Bahamas and the Lesser Antilles to Trinidad.

The *Spencer's* first twelve-day neutrality patrol began on November 15, 1939. With their glistening white hulls, the cutters displayed an oversized U.S. flag that was illuminated at night with the ship's powerful searchlights to prevent mistaking their identity. Ray recalled that the *Spencer* was in port for three weeks and then redeployed on its second patrol. On that deployment, both Doug and Ray were promoted to seaman second class and received a pay raise to thirty-six dollars per month.[22]

With the onset of the Neutrality Patrols, work on board the *Spencer* was never-ending. Patrols in the North Atlantic took a tremendous toll on the ship, the equipment, and the crew. In the treacherous North Atlantic waters, the *Spencer* and its crew faced two unrelenting enemies. First, the highly corrosive sea water ate away everything it touched. The crew was caught up in a continuous cycle of painting, preventative maintenance, and patrolling, followed by restorative maintenance and more painting. Second, the ever-present German U-boats constituted an ongoing threat.[23]

U-boats were constructed in several types and used quite effectively by the German navy against Allied shipping during World War II. Nearly unstoppable during the early stages of the war, U-boats sunk more than five thousand merchant ships carrying more than 13 million tons of cargo. Late in the war, Allied forces were able to design and effectively use countermeasures such as aircraft reconnaissance and depth changes.

Winter in the North Atlantic had to be experienced to be believed. With an average water temperature of forty-three degrees and below-freezing air temperatures, blowing water from the waves froze instantly on exposed skin and everything else. On deck, crewmen worked in rotations of five to ten minutes due to the extreme conditions. Frequent winter storms created swells of ten to thirty feet that crashed over the bow and obliterated the entire ship for several seconds. Anything or anyone not secured was swept overboard. On more than one occasion, the *Spencer* lost more than one of its lifeboats.[24]

The crashing waves coupled with the below-freezing air temperatures added layer upon layer of thick, treacherous ice on the

entire ship, including the mast. The weight of the ice severely com-
promised the ship's stability. It was an unending battle for the crew.
Secured by ropes and cables, crewmen climbed a narrow staircase
and beat the ice from the mast with baseball bats and steel bars,
then threw the large chunks of freed ice back into the sea. Entering
a storm was like moving into a churning, all-consuming white wall
that extended down to the surface of the water. Those on the mast,
high above the ship, could not see the deck below.[25]

Despite the weather conditions and the ever-present U-boats,
maritime safety and commerce remained one of the core missions
of the Coast Guard. Doug and Ray knew what was at stake. By
early May 1940, Hitler, in an apparent attempt to force an end to
the war, invaded France. To avoid the heavily defended Maginot
Line,[26] the Germans first attacked Belgium, the Netherlands, and
Luxembourg, creating a gateway for the invasion of France. Following Germany's swift and successful occupation of France and
the Low Countries in May 1940, Hitler grew impatient with Great
Britain's rejection of his peace overtures and announced the invasion of England.[27]

With much of Europe now under Nazi oppression, England
stood alone as the bulwark against Hitler's quest for world domination. The safety of Allied shipping in the North Atlantic was
imperative, as it carried provisions, food, matériel, and fuel to keep
England in the fight.

Beginning on July 10, 1940, the German Luftwaffe began 111
days of aerial attacks on targets throughout the United Kingdom.
The resulting struggle between the Germans and the British for air
superiority would later be called the Battle of Britain.

HAVING RETURNED FROM their second patrol, everyone on board the
Spencer listened as President Roosevelt, in a fireside chat on December 29, moved the United States a decisive step forward toward
war.[28] Also listening was James and Edith Munro, as well as most
everyone with access to a radio.[29] In his remarks, Roosevelt declared

that ". . . the Nazi masters of Germany have made it clear that they intend not only to dominate all life and thought in their own country, but also to enslave the whole of Europe, and then to use the resources of Europe to dominate the rest of the world."[30]

Doug and Ray looked at each other; they knew that the president, their commander in chief, had just brought the war in Europe right to the shores of the United States.[31] Men in uniform, regardless of service branch, saw the thunderclouds of war darken on the horizon. Back in Cle Elum, Edith Munro breathed a sigh of relief. Her thoughts turned to her extended family in Liverpool.[32]

Despite the steady drumbeat of war in Europe, Doug and Ray found time to enjoy New York City life. On New Year's Eve, they experienced the excitement in Times Square. While neither was shy, Doug's outgoing personality and infectious smile allowed him to make friends easily and in large numbers, especially among the ladies—which made him even more popular with his shipmates. Doug and Ray joined thousands of others in ringing in the New Year. Then they, along with many other crew members, returned to the ship just before dawn, in time to shower, shave, and report for duty.[33]

The *Spencer's* third and final patrol ended on January 26, 1940, the same day Doug and Ray were promoted to seaman first class and received a raise in pay to fifty four dollars per month.[34] The Grand Banks Neutrality Patrol was officially discontinued the following day. The long weeks at sea proved to be the best training for officers and crew, working them into a high state of readiness and efficiency. With daily repetition and practice, every task became second nature. Everyone worked together to anticipate each other while completing the hundreds of finely tuned and intricate procedures required on a multimission ship.

As the war continued to rage in Europe and the Atlantic, the flow of weather data from merchant ships stopped at a time when there was a dramatic increase in the number of American civilians evacuating Europe. While most departed by ocean liner, diplomats and those with financial means were evacuated by Pan American "Clippers," which departed from Lisbon, Portugal, and flew to New York via the Azores and Bermuda. In late January 1940, President Roosevelt tasked the Coast Guard, in cooperation with the U.S. Weather Bureau, with the creation of two weather observation stations, called ocean stations, between Bermuda and the Azores.[35]

Ocean station duty consisted of a cutter streaming continuously within a one hundred square mile area from the center of the station during a three-week rotation. In addition to providing critical weather data for the Pan Am pilots, the weather patrol cutters provided assistance to military aircraft in the form of navigational aid, air to ground to air communication and search-and-rescue operations.[36]

After embarking meteorologists from the Weather Bureau, the *Spencer* sailed for Ocean Station 2 on March 18. Ocean station duty resulted in almost total isolation. The stations were located far away from shipping lanes, so a cutter often completed a deployment without ever seeing another ship.

Twice each day, meteorologists released a helium-filled balloon approximately five feet in diameter. Depending on atmospheric conditions, red, white, or black balloons were used. While the rate of ascent was easily determined, gyro repeaters determined the azimuth and a mariner's astrolabe measured the altitude. The cloud ceiling was determined by the amount of time it took the balloon to disappear in the cloud cover. At midnight, a radio device that recorded temperature, pressure, and humidity was attached to a balloon and launched; it transmitted data until the balloon burst. Corrected for the ship's course and speed, the encoded findings were transmitted to the Army six times each day.[37]

The meteorologists were very busy, but for most of the crew, ocean station duty was torturous and monotonous. Doug and the rest of the crew were incommunicado with family and friends, and, due to the remote location, mail was rarely delivered until the end of the deployment.

However, Doug and Ray soon found a welcome diversion. At the end of World War I, the Coast Guard had all but abolished the signalman rating, the oldest sea service rating. Signalmen were responsible for transmitting, receiving, encoding, decoding, and distributing messages through the use of flags and visual Morse code. With the threat of war looming ever larger, the signalman rating became critical. Doug and Ray saw another opportunity and quickly volunteered to train as signalmen. While given permission to begin signalman training by Commander Harold S. Berdine, USCG, the *Spencer's* executive officer, it was made clear to both men that they were expected to continue their quartermaster duties.[38]

With the near abolishment of the rating went almost all of the instructors and equipment required to train new signalmen. As a result, the Gold Dust Twins had to be their own instructors. Despite their double workload and lack of instruction and equipment, they studied and practiced every day early into the morning hours on their own time after their assigned work shift. The workload and hours of training began to take their toll on both men. Ray utilized any downtime to catch up on sleep, but Doug began to suffer from incapacitating migraine headaches that required him to be confined to sick bay for two or three days at a time. After his release, Doug resumed the same brutal work and training schedules as before.[39]

Essentially stationary at sea hundreds of miles from the nearest port during the three-week rotation, Doug, Ray, and the rest of the crew were isolated except for the radio, which was intermittent and dependent on weather conditions. These were long and lonely times.[40] The only sounds were the endless waves against the ship's hull and the haunting low-frequency "songs" of the whales. On moonless nights, nothing could be seen. Ask any mariner, there is nothing darker than an overcast night at sea.

When the *Spencer* returned to port for resupply in mid-April, Doug received another letter from his sister informing him that she and Burt had married on April 5, in Seattle. The timing was perfect, as both Doug and Ray were granted leave. Both packed their bags and boarded a Greyhound bus for the four-day transcontinental journey to Seattle. Even though sitting on a bus for four days was boring, Doug and Ray welcomed the opportunity to relax, read, and catch up on sleep. Upon arriving in Seattle, they agreed to meet again in three weeks for their return to New York.[41]

Doug's parents and sister and her husband were at the station to welcome him and drive him home to South Cle Elum. Much to Doug's chagrin, he arrived home to find that the house was filled with family and friends. While he was most certainly glad to have the opportunity to see everyone, he would have preferred a quiet, uneventful return home.[42]

After a couple of days, the constant parade of visitors slowed and Doug had the opportunity to join Patricia for several ski trips to the mountains and spend some time with his friend Mike Cooley. A week after Doug arrived home, another friend, Dale Cox, returned to Cle Elum on leave from the Army. They spent several hours comparing stories and prognosticating about world events and discussing how their respective services were engaged in activities that led both to believe that the United States would enter the war.

Doug and his father spent several evenings strolling down the streets of Cle Elum. During their walks, they talked about recent world events.[43] Earlier in the month, Hitler had invaded both Denmark and Norway. Denmark had surrendered immediately. While Doug and Ray crossed the country, British troops occupied the Danish Faroe Islands, and both British and French troops began landing in Norway.

James, Doug, and Dale also spent a couple of evenings at the American Legion post. Someone was always handing them a drink, and each were toasted many times. Most of the time Doug sipped a single drink all evening and gave the others away.[44]

But, after a couple of weeks, Doug was restless. This did not go unnoticed by either of his parents. Several times during his stay, the three of them would leave town on day trips to Seattle. Doug also took the opportunity to decompress by hiking, skiing, and taking leisurely walks in the mountains.

The day before his parents drove him back to Seattle, Doug and Mike Cooley walked the three miles from South Cle Elum to Laurel Hill Cemetery. As they passed through the veteran's section, Doug reminisced that as a member of the Sons of the American Legion, he had played "Taps" there many times—too many to remember—to honor local veterans. The conversation on their walk back to town centered on world events and how things seemed to be spinning out of control. Soon the entire world would again be at war.[45]

Early the next day, Doug was up before dawn, packed and ready to return to Seattle. As James drove to the bus station, Doug brought his father up to date about the changes on board ship, the Neutrality Patrol, and ocean station duty. He reiterated the importance of the work they were doing but stated he felt that there was more that he could do and wanted to look for additional opportunities when he got back. The ninety-minute drive seemed to pass quickly.[46]

James pulled the car up in front of the Seattle Greyhound station. Doug quickly opened the car door, grabbed his bag, smiled at his father, turned, and walked into the building. Ray entered through another door. They exchanged pleasantries, then, with nearly an hour before their bus was scheduled to leave, decided to eat.[47]

Four days later, when they reported back on board the *Spencer*, they found several major changes to the ship, including the newest sonar and depth-charge technology to supplement the traditional deck guns and small-arms components. Within three days, the ship weighed anchor for another ocean station duty, and with it the opportunity for Doug and Ray to continue their signalman training.[48]

The *Spencer* served at Ocean Station 2 again in May–June, July–August, and September–October 1940. After the *Spencer* completed its October weather patrol, the Navy ordered the ship to the Bethlehem Shipbuilding Corporation for further equipment upgrades to the depth-charge racks, the Y-gun (a two-barreled anti-submarine weapon shaped like the letter "Y" that was used to throw depth charges to either side of the stern), and the sonar equipment. This rearmament process lasted until mid-December, at which time the *Spencer* received orders to Ocean Station 1 and reentered the ocean station rotation.

In September 1940, both Doug and Ray earned their signal-man ratings and were promoted to signalman third class.[49] Signal-men stood watch on signal bridges, and sent and received messages by flashing light and semaphore. They prepared headings and ad-dresses for outgoing messages; processed messages; encoded and decoded message headings; operated voice radio; maintained visual signal equipment; rendered passing honors to ships and boats; and displayed ensigns and personal flags during salutes and colors. They also performed duties as lookouts; sent and received visual recognition signals; repaired signal flags, pennants, and ensigns; took bearings; and served as navigator's assistants.

That September, while much of the world was already at war, Congress passed the Selective Training and Service Act, the first peacetime conscription law ever enacted.[50] Doug's prediction had proved true. The law provided for the annual induction of nine hundred thousand men between the ages of twenty-one and thirty-six. The following month, more than 16 million men registered. At that time, the Army was the only armed service taking draftees; however, many nondraftees looked for alternatives, and joined the ranks of the Navy or the Coast Guard. With the nation's economy still within the grips of the Great Depression, the promise of three meals a day and a dry bed was more appealing than the city streets or a muddy foxhole.

1941: WAR ON THE HORIZON

American, Canadian, and British military leaders met in Washington, D.C., from January 29 through March 27, 1941, to debate what the strategic goal would be if the United States entered the war. At the conclusion of the conference, two important agreements were made: First, the primary goal of the Allied war effort was to defeat Germany; and second, if the United States entered the war, the Atlantic Fleet would help the British Royal Navy convoy ships across the Atlantic.

In March 1941, Congress enacted Lend-Lease Act, which allowed the United States to sell weapons to Allied countries and ended the public pretense that the country was a neutral party. On March 27–29, British naval forces defeated Italy in the Battle of Cape Matapan off the southwest coast of Greece's Peloponnesian peninsula.[51] The German Luftwaffe all but obliterated the city of Swansea, South Wales, after three intensive nights of bombing in April.

As a consequence of the Nazi invasion of Denmark the previous year, President Roosevelt and his military leaders were concerned that the Danish-owned island of Greenland would soon be under Hitler's control. Located between Canada and Iceland in the North Atlantic, Greenland is the largest island in the world and located almost entirely within the Arctic Circle. In addition to its strategic geographic location, Greenland was valuable because it contained large quantities of cryolite, a mineral used in the production of aluminum. In an agreement with the exiled Danish government, the United States assumed responsibility for the defense of Greenland, which already housed American military bases. The Coast Guard organized and conducted patrol operations around Greenland.[52]

On May 27, 1941, Doug, Ray, and the entire crew of the *Spencer* listened as President Roosevelt again took to the airwaves and declared an unlimited national emergency. He stated, "The war is approaching the brink of the Western Hemisphere itself. It is coming very close to home . . . The Battle of the Atlantic now extends from the icy waters of the North Pole to the frozen continent of the Antarctic."[53] The president noted that a large number of Axis raiders and submarines had actually been detected within the waters of the Western Hemisphere and declared that "it would be suicide to wait until they are in our front yard . . . old-fashioned common sense calls for the use of a strategy which will prevent such an enemy from gaining a foothold in the first place. We have, accordingly, extended our patrol in North and South Atlantic waters. We are steadily adding more and more ships and planes to that patrol."[54] The same day the president spoke to the nation, the Royal Navy torpedoed and sunk the German battleship *Bismarck* in the North Atlantic.

The world situation continued to deteriorate. Japan signed a neutrality pact with the Soviet Union on April 13. The American government froze all German and Italian assets in the United States, and Germany invaded the Soviet Union on June 22. In response to the Japanese occupation of French Indochina in September 1940, on June 14, Roosevelt ordered the assets of the Japanese government in the United States seized and instituted an embargo of American oil, steel, and other strategic exports to Japan in an attempt to slow its war-making capabilities, and warned the Japanese government against invading Thailand in the future.

As spring turned to summer, the U.S. military continued to prepare for war. The Navy assumed control over several Army troop transports left over from World War I, along with several other passenger ships capable of moving large numbers of troops and equipment. The drums of war became louder. There was a long-standing sentiment in the American military that something was about to happen, but there was no strong consensus as to what, when, or where. Congress approved the Two-Ocean Navy Act, which increased naval procurement by 70 percent.[55]

During the summer of 1941, war with Germany, if not with Japan as well, had taken on an air of inevitability. Newspapers and magazines of this period were filled with stories of a buildup of

American military forces and FDR's slow but steady ramping up of what later would be called the military-industrial complex.

During this same period of time, both Doug and Ray had tired of duty in the North Atlantic and were looking for another opportunity. Both men had been promoted to Signalman second class in May.[56] Now they learned that President Roosevelt had ordered the Coast Guard to man four large transport ships and serve in mixed crews on board twenty-two Navy ships, all of which needed signalmen. Doug and Ray looked at each other and smiled. This was a once-in-a-lifetime opportunity, and neither man had any intention of letting it pass them by. Together, Doug and Ray approached Commander Berdine, the *Spencer*'s executive officer, and requested transfers to the USS *Hunter Liggett*, a Navy ship under the command of a Coast Guard captain.[57] Their request met with some resistance, according to Ray. Both he and Doug "harassed" the commander for the transfer, but he kept replying, "I can't let both of you go at once." Over the next several days, both men ramped up their verbal efforts. Ray recalled, "We harassed him until he finally just gave up and said, 'OK, both of you get out of here!'"[58]

The USS *Hunter Liggett* was a 535-foot *Harris*-class attack transport named in honor of a former Army general. Originally built as the *SS Pan America* in 1922, it served many years as a transatlantic passenger ship. The ship was acquired by the Army and renamed in February 1939; it operated as a transport until May 1941, when it was transferred to the Navy and converted for naval use at the Brooklyn Navy Yard. It was subsequently commissioned as *AP-27* on June 9, 1941, under the command of Captain Louis W. Perkins, USCG.

Doug Munro and Ray Evans joined the crew of 52 officers and more than 650 enlisted men. At the time of their transfer, both believed that they were to be a part of the ship's company, but they soon learned that they were assigned to the commander of Transport Division 17, Commodore G. B. Ashe. All of the staff officers were Navy except for Commander Dwight H. Dexter, who served as personnel officer. The majority of the personnel on the vessels in the transport division, both officers and men, were Coast Guardsmen, affectionately known as "coasties." The *Liggett* served as the flagship of the transport division.[59]

Once the men were on board and all modifications to the ship were completed, the *Hunter Liggett* sailed for Onslow Bay, located along the coast of North Carolina, along with the other transports in the division: the USS *Dickman*, the USS *Leonard Wood*, the USS *Wakefield*, the USS *Alcyone*, and the USS *Betelgeuse*. Each of the transport ships carried a large number of unique amphibious landing craft known as Higgins boats. In early 1941, the Marine Corps had developed the doctrine of amphibious warfare, which was designed to take Allied forces successfully over every beachhead. During previous joint exercises, it had become clear to military leaders that specialized crews would be required to handle the task of successfully inserting and extracting landing craft from the beaches. While the Navy had adopted the use of the Higgins boats for its anticipated landings on the beaches of North Africa, France, and the South Pacific, "Navy crews proved frustratingly inept in maneuvering the newly designed landing craft in the surf . . . Coast Guardsmen had been expertly manning small craft in the surf zone since before the establishment of the U.S. Life Saving Service in 1871 and were the most seasoned small boat handlers in government service." The Navy and the Army asked the Coast Guard to assist in what would become one of its most important roles during World War II.[60]

In addition to manning landing craft and instructing others about their operation, the Coast Guard also assumed the role of operating the Army-owned attack transports that had been subsequently transferred to the Navy.[61]

At the end of July, the transport division arrived at Onslow Bay. Onslow Bay, located between Cape Lookout in the north and Cape Fear in the south, is an indentation in the North Carolina coast with thirteen barrier islands forming the shore of the bay. Its strong, sustained winds create consistent waves of two to three feet, perfect for the repeated practice of beach and surf landings. The coasties took advantage of these drills to demonstrate their expertise as small-boat coxswains on the undeveloped beaches.

For the seasoned coasties who were well versed in the handling of small boats, the Higgins boats and the landing conditions proved to be of little challenge. They were inherently more skillful, more resourceful, and more in their element in small boats than their Navy counterparts, who were much more accustomed to maneuvering large boats and ships. This resulted in good-natured ribbing between the two services, but under the tutelage of the coasties, the Navy coxswains soon could more than hold their own. Despite having no prior small-boat experience, both Doug and Ray, seeing yet another opportunity in the critical shortage of trained coxswains, requested and received permission to join the training.

During the summer, the coxswains practiced small-boat maneuvers in open water. The *Liggett* and its sister ships moved to Solomon's Island, located north of the mouth of the Patuxent River, where it joins Chesapeake Bay. Here, procedures for debarking troops from the transports to the Higgins landing craft were practiced, as well as boat maneuvering, surf landings, and consolidation of cargo on the beaches.

Ray later claimed that he had become a good coxswain, but "Doug was much better, he just had that instinct . . . that touch. I'm not sure what it was, but Doug had it. He was a natural."[62]

THE FINAL CALM BEFORE THE STORM

On August 15, the command of Transport Division 17 was transferred from the *Liggett* to the USS *Dickman*. Doug and Ray packed their bags and joined the division's commander and staff officers on board the *Dickman*, which then proceeded to the Brooklyn Navy Yard for overhaul and weapons upgrade. The *Dickman* was built as the *Peninsula State* for the United States Shipping Board by the New York Shipbuilding Corporation of Camden,

New Jersey, in 1921. A multimission agency, the United Shipping Board was established on September 7, 1916, to regulate commercial maritime carriers and trade practices and transfers of ship's registry. The agency was abolished in 1934. The ship, renamed the *President Roosevelt*, began transatlantic passenger service in 1922. It was acquired by the War Department in 1940 and renamed the *Dickman* under the command of Lieutenant Commander Charles W. Harwood, USCG.

In early August 1941, President Roosevelt and British prime minister Winston Churchill met in Argentia, Newfoundland, and created the pivotal Atlantic Charter. Issued as a joint declaration, it detailed the goals and aims of the Allied powers regarding the war and the postwar world. It clarified any question that the United States was in full support of Great Britain. The charter was of particular interest and comfort to the Munro family, as Edith had many relatives in England.[63]

Despite their duties as signalmen and budding coxswains, Doug and Ray, along with the other crew members, maintained backbreaking dawn-to-dusk work schedules while assisting with the wartime modifications to the ship. However, weekends meant well-deserved liberty, and for the next six weeks, the *Dickman* saw neither Doug nor Ray until work call on Monday mornings.

Following successful post-modification testing in Narragansett Bay, the *Dickman* proceeded to Hampton Roads, Virginia, where intense practice drills were conducted in Chesapeake Bay. Through these practice drills, Doug mastered the art of small-boat maneuvering and began making a name for himself in both Navy and Coast Guard circles. Though he was involved in serious and strenuous work, Doug was having the time of his life. Ray recalled, "His enthusiasm clearly showed."[64]

In October, Germany began an all-out assault against the Soviet Union in an effort to capture Moscow before the onset of winter. On October 17, while the USS *Kearny*, a *Benson-Livermore*-class destroyer, was docked at Reykjavík, Iceland, before America's formal entry into the war, it was called upon to assist a convoy whose Canadian escorts were being overwhelmed. The ship was hit by on the starboard side by a German U-boat torpedo. The *Kearny* lost eleven men, and twenty-two others were injured, but the ship was able to safely return to Iceland for emergency repairs.

Also based in Iceland was the USS *Reuben James*, a *Clemson*-class destroyer. On October 31, while escorting a convoy, the *Reuben James* was torpedoed by a German U-boat after it had positioned itself between an ammunition ship in the convoy and the known position of the submarine. The entire bow was blown off when a magazine exploded. The bow sank immediately, but the aft section floated for five minutes before going down. Of the nearly 160-man crew, only 44 survived. The *Reuben James* was the first U.S. Navy ship lost in World War II.

The *Dickman*, along with the *Leonard Wood*, the *Orizaba*, the *Mt. Vernon*, the *West Point*, and the *Wakefield*, weighed anchor for Halifax, Nova Scotia, on November 2, one day after both Doug and Ray received promotions to signalman first class. Arriving on the sixth, the flag of Transport Division 17 was transferred to the *Leonard Wood*, which meant Doug and Ray had to pack their bags once more and engage in another round of good-byes. Doug jokingly suggested that when they boarded the *Leonard Wood* that they should forgo unpacking and just live out of their duffels.[65]

The *Leonard Wood*, formerly named the *Nutmeg State* and the *Western World*, had also served as a passenger liner at one time. It had been acquired in 1939 by the War Department and was renamed after a former Army chief of staff. The ship was manned by Coast Guardsmen with Commander H. G. Bradbury, USCG, in command. Boarding the *Leonard Wood* with Doug and Ray were fifteen hundred troops. Equal numbers of troops boarded the other transports.

Transport Division 17 departed Halifax on November 10 and proceeded south. Its destination was Bombay, India, where the troops would disembark. On the same date, Joseph Grew, the U.S.

ambassador to Japan, cabled the State Department that the Japanese had plans to launch an attack against Pearl Harbor. His warning apparently went ignored—a critical mistake, given subsequent events. Unbeknownst to U.S. political and military leaders, an Imperial Japanese Navy (IJN) attack fleet of thirty-three warships set sail for the Hawaiian Islands on November 26, the same day that Secretary of State Cordell Hull had delivered a note, officially known as the *Outline of Proposed Basis for Agreement Between the United States and Japan*, to the Japanese authorities. On November 27, based on intercepts of Japanese messages, both the War and Navy departments sent a "war warning" to all commands: "Negotiations with Japan looking toward stabilization of conditions in the Pacific have ceased and an aggressive move by Japan is expected within the next few days."[66]

As the transports rounded the Cape of Good Hope on Sunday, December 7, 1941, the public address system on each ship announced the news that the IJN had attacked the Pacific Fleet of the U.S. Navy.[67] Throughout the day, news outlets reported the carnage and devastation. Everyone on board knew that American involvement in the war had not been not a matter of if, only when; they had been waiting on the circumstance. December 7 was the when; Pearl Harbor was the circumstance.

The mood of the troops on board the *Dickman* was very somber; little talking was heard. According to Ray, "As casualty reports began being released, the mood changed from shock to anger. A quiet resolve seemed to come over us. No one had to tell us, we were at war."[68]

As later reports were released, personnel losses were severe. The Navy had 2,008 killed, 710 wounded; the Army, 218 killed, 364 wounded; the Marines, 109 killed, 69 wounded. Sixty-eight civilians were killed, and 35 were wounded.

Ship damage ran the gamut. Of the battleships stationed at Pearl, the *Arizona,* the *California*, and the *West Virginia* had been sunk; the *Oklahoma* had capsized; the Nevada was heavily damaged;

and the *Maryland*, the *Tennessee*, and the *Pennsylvania* were damaged. As each ship's name was announced, grimaces appeared on the crew's faces, and shouts of anger were heard. But the reports kept coming. The destroyers *Cassin, Downes, Shaw*, and *Helm* were damaged. The cruisers *Helena, Raleigh*, and *Honolulu* were damaged. The minesweeper *Oglala* had been sunk. Among auxiliary ships, the *Curtiss* was damaged, the *Sotoyomo* and the *Utah* were sunk, and the *Vestal* was heavily damaged, while the floating dry dock *YFD-2* was sunk.

And just when the crew thought they had heard enough, the aircraft damage reports came: the Navy had lost 92 aircraft lost, with 31 damaged; the Army Air Corps suffered 77 planes lost, with 128 damaged. Most of the aircraft losses were sustained while the planes were still parked on their tarmacs.[69]

Knowing that the Coast Guard had a strong presence at Pearl Harbor, Doug and Ray looked at each other. Doug asked, "What about us? What about the Coast Guard?"[70] Ray shrugged his shoulders.

THE COAST GUARD indeed had a strong presence in Hawaii. Cutters were assigned to ocean patrol, port security, search and rescue, and aids to navigation duties before December 7, 1941. During the IJN attack, Coast Guard ships and personnel responded with weapons fire; covered and escorted private watercraft, fishing boats, and cruise ships out of the harbor's restricted areas; and impounded suspicious vessels.[71]

Commander John Wooley, USN, commanded the Inshore Patrol Command, which included four Navy destroyers, four Navy minesweepers, and three Coast Guard cutters: the USS *Taney*, the USS *Tiger*, and the USS *Reliance*. The cutters were charged with patrolling shoreline areas to prevent espionage and the transfer and landing of illegal contraband and people.

When the Coast Guard became part of the Navy on November 1, 1941, its cutters were assigned submarine-tracking duties in the Atlantic, the Pacific, and the Gulf of Mexico. To carry out these duties, the cutters were equipped with the latest classified sonar technology to supplement their traditional deck guns and small-arms complement.[72]

The *Taney*, under the command of Commander G. B. Gelly, was a destroyer-sized 327-foot cutter with a 41-foot beam and a 2,216-ton displacement. Its armament included several .50-caliber machine guns and six 3-inch and six 5-inch guns. Moored at its homeport at Pier 6 in Honolulu, six miles from the main Navy anchorage at Pearl Harbor, during the first wave of the IJN attack, the *Taney* pulled away from the pier. The crew had gone to general quarters at their first sight of the attacking planes and commenced firing as the second wave passed overhead.[73]

Other Coast Guard craft assigned to Pearl Harbor were the 190-foot buoy tender *Kukui*, under the command of Chief Warrant Officer William J. Mazzoni; the 125-foot patrol craft *Tiger* and *Reliance*, the 78-foot cutters *CG-400* and *CG-403*; the 60-foot *CG-27*; *CG-4818*; and *CG-517*, a small buoy boat. Ships unable to fight immediately initiated search-and-rescue efforts. That fateful day, Coast Guardsmen pulled hundreds of burned and oil-covered men from what appeared to be a sea of fire, wounded from damaged ships, and bodies from the water.[74]

CHAPTER 4

THE SOUTH PACIFIC

After December 7, 1941, the *Leonard Wood* took on a whole new life. According to Ray, "Tasks and duties that had become routine were no longer routine, the laughing and joking on board subsided, without instruction everyone aboard took their performance up several notches. We were at war, it just had not been declared . . . yet."[1]

The next day, the entire crew and troops stood quietly and listened to the closest public address speaker as President Roosevelt spoke before a joint session of Congress.

> *"Mr. Vice President, Mr. Speaker, members of the Senate, and of the House of Representatives:*
> *"Yesterday, December 7, 1941, a date which will live in infamy, the United States of America was suddenly and deliberately attacked by naval and air forces of the Empire of Japan."*

Doug and Ray just stood motionless with the others, each keeping his thoughts to himself as President Roosevelt continued.[2] They could hear his words, but their minds were elsewhere. After what seemed like an eternity, all were mentally snapped back to the present when the president said, "I ask that the Congress declare that since the unprovoked and dastardly attack by Japan on Sunday, December 7, 1941, a state of war has existed between the United States and the Japanese empire."

Following the president's speech and the subsequent declaration of war, the crew learned from news updates that in addition to the attack on Pearl Harbor, the IJN had bombed Hong Kong, Singapore, Malaya, Thailand, the Philippines, and Shanghai.

During the month of December 1941, the world continued on a rapid downward spiral toward global conflict. Germany and Italy declared war on the United States; America reciprocated on December 11, 1941. The first Japanese landing attack on Wake Island was repelled. India and China declared war on Japan. The IJN invaded Borneo and landed on Hong Kong, which soon surrendered. The IJN's second attack on Wake Island was successful after heavy fighting. The siege of Sevastopol, a port city in the Crimea on the Black Sea, began along Europe's eastern front. British commandos raided the Russian port, causing Hitler to reinforce the garrison and strengthen its defenses.

When the *Leonard Wood* arrived in India, security was extremely tight. Troops and equipment were quickly unloaded under the watchful eye of heavily armed soldiers. After all matériel and troops were off-loaded, the *Leonard Wood* returned to the Philadelphia Navy Yard to be converted into an amphibious attack transport. Doug and Ray remained on the *Leonard Wood* until April 2, 1942, when Transport Division 17's flag was transferred back to the *Hunter Liggett*.

Carrying 1,461 troops, 12 nurses, and a civilian in addition to the crew, the *Liggett* departed New York on April 9 with the rest of the transport division. After a one-week layover at Balboa, in the

Canal Zone, to complete some overhaul work, they sailed on to Wellington, New Zealand, arriving on May 28. The nearly sixty-day trip was not a pleasure cruise for the crew. The days were long and strenuous, as the Higgins boats and the ships required constant maintenance.

STRATEGIC BACKGROUND

Beginning in January 1941, a series of conferences between the combined sea, ground, and air chiefs of staff of the United States and Great Britain had been conducted to discuss various strategies to defeat the Axis Powers.[3] As a result of these conferences, a list of priorities was established to guide British and American war efforts once the United States entered the conflict. Because the United States was officially neutral when these conferences began, the two Atlantic partners referred to themselves as the Associated Powers.

Both of the conferees agreed on a Germany-first strategy.[4] The anti-Axis coalition would concentrate its efforts on defeating Adolph Hitler's Nazi Third Reich and Benito Mussolini's Fascist Italy before turning its focus on Japan. Until the war in Europe was successfully completed, the Associated Powers could only execute a "containment" strategy against the Empire of Japan.[5] Consistent with the Germany-first policy, the war planners divided the world into various geographical regions, with each of the Associated Powers responsible for different designated regions. The British would focus on the western European and Mediterranean theaters, while the United States would carry the burden of mounting limited offenses against Japan in the Pacific.[6]

On January 27, the U.S. ambassador to Japan, Joseph C. Grew, wired Washington that he had learned that Japan was planning a surprise attack on Pearl Harbor. Grew's report made it to Chief of Naval Operations Harold R. Stark and subsequently to the newly appointed commander at Pearl Harbor. Reportedly, most senior military experts believed that the Japanese would attack Manila in the Philippines Islands if war broke out. Grew's report was discarded.

On February 1, 1941, Admiral Husband E. Kimmel assumed command of the U.S. Pacific Fleet in Hawaii. Within weeks, he asked the War Department for additional personnel and equipment to properly defend the military installations under his watch. On September 24, U.S. intelligence officials deciphered a "bomb plot" message to Japan's consul general in Honolulu that requested a map containing the exact locations of the ships in Pearl Harbor. The information was not shared with Pearl Harbor's military leaders.

Within a month following the devastating blow administered by the Japanese navy at Pearl Harbor, both the IJN and the IJA moved quickly to exert complete Japanese domination over eastern Asia and the western Pacific. By the middle of January 1942, Japan had taken control of Burma and established bases in New Britain and the northern Solomon Islands.[7] Japanese occupation of Singapore, Sumatra, and Java followed in February.

However, Admiral Ernest J. King, the fiery commander in chief of the entire U.S. Fleet who also served as chief of naval operations and was member of the Joint Chiefs of Staff, scoffed at the idea of containing Japan until the war in Europe had been concluded.[8] King argued that Japan had crippled the U.S. Pacific Fleet, driven Britain from the Indian Ocean, taken Wake Island and Guam, and broken the "unbreakable" Malay Barrier and was now threatening to invade New Guinea. King knew that the Japanese invasion force was being gathered at Rabaul at the eastern tip of New Britain.[9] With the exception of occasional American strikes against the Gilbert and Marshall Islands, the entire Pacific Ocean was in danger of becoming a Japanese lake.[10] King believed that the United States could not wait for an Allied victory in Europe before decisively taking action against Japan. A month after Pearl Harbor, King ordered American troops to garrison Fiji.[11]

The United States assumed the responsibility for the Pacific Ocean and tasked Admiral Chester W. Nimitz, commander in chief of the Pacific Fleet, with the job of winning the Pacific back from the Japanese.[12] On March 30, 1942, the U.S. Joint chiefs of

Staff divided the Pacific theater of operations into three areas: the Pacific Ocean Areas, the South West Pacific Area, and the Southeast Pacific Area.

ADMIRAL CHESTER WILLIAM Nimitz was born on February 24, 1885, in Fredericksburg, Texas. As a young man, he had set his sights on an Army career and unsuccessfully sought an appointment to the U.S. Military Academy at West Point. Turning his attention to the sea, he received an appointment to the U.S. Naval Academy at Annapolis in 1901. After graduating from high school, he joined the Class of 1905. He graduated with distinction, 14th in a class of 144. After serving in various billets and commands, he attended the Naval War College in Newport, Rhode Island. Upon graduation, he was assigned as the chief of staff to Admiral Samuel Shelburne Robison, then commander in chief of the U.S. Fleet. Immediately following the attack on Pearl Harbor, Nimitz served in the dual role of commander in chief of the Pacific Fleet and the Pacific Ocean Areas.[13]

ADMIRAL KING ALSO knew that the Royal Australian Navy (RAN) had expanded the coastwatchers, a unique group of resourceful and courageous men who operated inside Japanese-controlled territory and reported on IJN activity.[14] Originally established by the Australian Commonwealth Board in 1922, the coastwatcher network at first operated exclusively along the Australian coastline; however, the aggressive actions of the Japanese resulted in the Fiji and Solomon Islands being added to the area of operations in 1939. Under the command of Lieutenant Commander Eric Feldt, RAN, the coastwatchers were taught radio communications using "Bull" code, a high-grade cipher code.[15] By the end of March, the network of coastwatchers, who skillfully evaded Japanese patrols and relayed critical intelligence information to the Allied Intelligence Bureau headquartered out of Australia, extended from New Ireland, in the Bismarck Archipelago, down to San Cristoval, at the southern tip of the Solomons. On the island of Guadalcanal, the coastwatcher was Martin Clemens, who until recently had been the district administrator for the Solomon Islands.[16]

On April 9, the Japanese Army defeated the U.S. Army at Bataan. Following the fall of the island of Corrigedor, on May 6, Lieutenant General Jonathan Wainwright surrendered all U.S. forces in the Philippines. Several days prior to the surrender, Japan established a base on Tulagi, a small island just off Florida Island in the southern Solomons. The U.S. Army assumed operational control of the Southwest Pacific Area under the command of General Douglas MacArthur, recently evacuated from the Philippines to Australia.

GENERAL DOUGLAS A. MacArthur was born on January 26, 1880, in Little Rock, Arkansas. Reared in a military family, MacArthur was valedictorian at the West Texas Military Academy and First Captain at West Point, where he graduated top of his class in 1903. In 1917, MacArthur was promoted to colonel and became the chief of staff of the 42nd ("Rainbow") Division. Fighting on the western front in World War I, he rose to the rank of brigadier general and was nominated for the Medal of Honor. He was subsequently awarded the Distinguished Service Cross twice and the Silver Star seven times. MacArthur was promoted again on January 17, 1925, becoming the Army's youngest major general. He became the chief of staff for the Army in 1930, and subsequently retired from active service in 1937.

MacArthur was recalled to active duty in 1941 and named as the commander of U.S. Army Forces in the Far East. In March 1942, he was ordered by President Truman to withdraw from the Philippines to Australia, where he became the Supreme Allied Commander of the South West Pacific Area on April 18, 1942. He was awarded the Medal of Honor for his defense of the Philippines.

ON APRIL 20, 1942, the Joint Chiefs further divided the Pacific Ocean Areas into the North, Central and South Pacific Areas.

Nimitz appointed Rear Admiral Robert A. Theobald as commander of the North Pacific Area; retained the Central Pacific Area, including Hawaii, under his direct command; and appointed Vice Admiral Robert L. Ghormley, as commander of the South Pacific Area, which included New Zealand, critical island bases at the end of the South Pacific ferry route, and the Solomon Islands, a former British protectorate five hundred miles from New Guinea. Ghormley's mission was to block the Japanese before they could cut the South Pacific ferry route and sever supply and communication lines between Australia and New Zealand and the United States.

VICE ADMIRAL ROBERT Lee Ghormley was born on October 15, 1883, in Portland, Oregon. A member of the Naval Academy's Class of 1906, he was commissioned an ensign in 1908 and advanced through the ranks to vice admiral. On June 19, 1942, he was named commander of the South Pacific Area and South Pacific Force.

HAVING DRIVEN THE American out of the Philippines, the British out of British Malaya, and the Dutch out of the East Indies, the Japanese began to expand into the western Pacific, taking islands in an attempt to build a defensive ring around their newly acquired territory and threaten the lines of communication from the U.S. to Australia and New Zealand. The Japanese reached Tulagi on May 3, when an IJN invasion force landed on an empty beach along the harbor. Clemens promptly radioed a report about the occupation to the Allied Intelligence Bureau in Townsville, Australia. The news that the Japanese were building a base on Tulagi drew a quick response from the U.S. Navy. On May 4, 1942, the carrier *Yorktown* launched three consecutive air attacks on the IJN at Tulagi. Clemens witnessed and reported on the attack from the shores of Aola Bay, across the channel.

Corregidor, the last remaining American stronghold in the Philippines, fell on May 6. News of the island fortress's surrender was soon followed by reports of the strategic American naval victory in the Coral Sea on May 4-8. But that far-ranging sea battle did little to diminish the enemy advance toward New Zealand and Australia, which further menaced Allied lines of communication in the South Pacific. While the U.S. Pacific Fleet at Pearl Harbor was being salvaged and repaired, reinforcements were consolidated in the southwestern Pacific to halt the Japanese advance by an attack on the Solomons.[17] The two primary objectives established were Tulagi and another small island just off Florida Island, Gavutu, where governmental buildings and the Lever Brothers plantation headquarters provided modern buildings and equipment that could be converted into important military assets.

On May 28, Clemens reported that a Japanese scouting party from Tulagi had landed at Lunga Point, midway on the northern coast of Guadalcanal. The IJN soon constructed a wharf there. On July 5, Clemens reported to Lieutenant Commander Feldt that the Japanese were burning off the tall kunai grass in the plains behind Lunga's cocoanut groves and constructing an airfield.[18] Feldt immediately transmitted the message to Washington, D.C.

Upon receiving Feldt's report, a new sense of urgency was felt by U.S. war planners. Admiral King and General George C. Marshall, the Army's chief of staff, had previously drafted a plan that would dispatch U.S. forces into the South Pacific with the overall objective of capturing Rabaul, the primary Japanese base in New Britain. Military strategists could clearly see that an airstrip on Guadalcanal would allow Japanese planes to threaten the sea lanes to Australia.

GENERAL MARSHALL WAS somewhat of an anomaly in the U.S. Army, which was dominated by West Point graduates. He graduated from the Virginia Military Institute with a commission as a second lieutenant in 1901. Marshall served in several infantry units and came to the attention of commanding general John J. Pershing, who became his mentor and made Marshall a member of his staff after World War I. He received his promotion to brigadier general in 1936. Three years later, President Roosevelt promoted Marshall over the heads of thirty-four officers more senior than him to become Army chief of staff.

THE FIRST PHASE of the plan had been the seizure of Tulagi and adjacent islands, but the Clemens dispatch changed the focus of America's first major offensive of the war. Guadalcanal became the new primary objective in the South Pacific.

The Spanish explorer Álvaro de Mendaña and his expedition passed through the Solomons in April 1568 and named Guadalcanal after a small town in Andalusia north of Seville in honor of Pedro del Ortega Valencia, a member of Mendaña's expedition. During the eighteenth and nineteenth centuries, European settlers and missionaries arrived in the island chain. In 1893, the United Kingdom established a protectorate over the Solomon Islands.

As the IJN converged on Australia from the north and the west, it became clear to the Allies, especially the Joint Chiefs of Staff, that the IJA was also involved in a pincer movement toward the island continent. Allied war planners now recognized that more than a mere show of force would have to be deployed against the Japanese just to contain them.

Although Vice Admiral Ghormley was the commander of all Allied forces in the South Pacific Area, Major General Alexander A. Vandegrift was tapped to lead the invasion of Guadalcanal as the commander of the 1st Marine Division, which had reached New Zealand on June 14.

MAJOR GENERAL ALEXANDER Archer Vandegrift was born in Charlottesville, Virginia, on March 13, 1887. While attending the University of Virginia in 1908, he successfully completed a weeklong competitive examination and was commissioned as a second lieutenant in the Marine Corps on January 22, 1909. He was promoted through the ranks, filling progressively demanding billets and commands. General Vandegrift was assigned to the 1st Marine Division in November 1941. Following his promotion to major general in March 1942, he sailed for the South Pacific.

ON JULY 21, 1942, the IJN landed IJA troops at Buna in a movement down the east coast of New Guinea matching the Japanese advance in the Solomons. Airstrips for land-based planes were constructed at Rabaul; at Kieta, on Bougainville; and on Guadalcanal. Seaplane bases were also established at Gavutu; at Gizo, off the coast of New Georgia; at Rekata Bay, on Santa Isabel Island; at Kieta; and along the Buka Passage, a narrow strait that separates Buku Island from the northern part of Bougainville Island. As a result, Allied convoys bound for Australia were now exposed to both torpedo and bombing attacks.

In mid-July, intelligence reports derived from Clemens's transmissions and reconnaissance flights reported the Japanese had 1,850 men in the Tulagi area and 5,275 on Guadalcanal. Although IJN ships and carriers had not been seen in the area since the Battle of the Coral Sea, quick action was necessary to prevent the IJN from reinforcing its positions on those islands. On July 23, 1942, the Joint Chiefs of Staff authorized Operation Watchtower, the seizure of Guadalcanal and Tulagi.

The plan called for American forces under the command of General MacArthur to interdict IJN activities west of the theater of operations with submarines and planes. The South Pacific Force, under the command of Admiral Ghormley, was ordered to occupy Tulagi and environs and also to seize the Santa Cruz Islands, which lie approximately 250 miles southeast of the Solomon Islands archipelago, to keep them out of Japanese control. To accomplish these tasks, three major task forces were created. The first, Task Force Negat, was to supply aircraft carrier support for the mission. The second, Task Force Tare, or Amphibious Force, was to make the principal attack, transporting and landing the Marines and defending the transport convoys from surface attack.

The third, Task Force Mike, was to provide aerial scouting and advance bombing of the islands. Included in the Amphibious Force was the *Hunter Liggett*.

War in the Pacific came with its own set of inherent problems. Covering 85 million square miles, the Pacific Ocean is twice the size of the Atlantic, is larger than the remaining four oceans combined, and occupies an area greater than the total area of all of Earth's landmasses; it also holds more than half of the planet's water at an average depth of fourteen thousand feet. During World War II, it became the battleground for the largest naval forces ever assembled. For Doug and Ray, the Pacific was an incredible sight.

There was little time for sightseeing. Duty hours were long and intense. Watches for Japanese subs were increased and constant. During off-duty time and in between news updates, Doug, Ray, and the rest of the crew on board the *Hunter Liggett* listened to radio broadcasts of the most popular artist of the time, Glenn Miller, which included his hit songs "String of Pearls," "Moonlight Serenade," and "Chattanooga Choo Choo."

WELLINGTON, NEW ZEALAND

Located at the southwestern tip of the North Island, Wellington is New Zealand's capital and was the staging area for Marine Corps operations in the South Pacific. As the *Hunter Liggett* entered Port Nicholson and arrived at the Queen's Wharf on May 28, Ray recalled, a large band was playing John Philip Sousa's "Stars and Stripes Forever." There were "cheering people everywhere, some waving American flags. The mayor of the city welcomed us. It really was quite something."[19] After disembarking the ship, many of the troops and crew on board the *Liggett* participated in a parade down Queen Street. Many local shops and stores displayed American flags and Rosie the Riveter posters in their front windows.

Upon its arrival in Wellington, the transport division's flag was transferred to the USS *Neville*, which was already in port along with several other ships. The *Neville* was a *Heywood*-class attack transport in the U.S. Navy. It was named for Wendell Cushing Neville, a general in the U.S. Marine Corps and its fourteenth commandant, serving in that post from 1920 to 1930. Originally built as a three-mast, 440-foot screw steamer named the USS *Independence* in 1918 by the Bethlehem Shipbuilding Corporation in Alameda, California, for the United States Shipping Board, it was commissioned on November 18, 1918. After service during World War I, it was decommissioned on March 20, 1919, and returned to the USSB for U.S. Merchant Marine service. Rebuilt and renamed the *City of Norfolk* in 1930, it was run by the Baltimore Mail Steamship Company until reacquired by the Navy on December 14, 1940. Converted to an attack transport by the Willamette Iron and Steel Works in Portland, Oregon, it was recommissioned as the *Neville* on May 14, 1941, under the command of Captain C. A. Bailey.

Arriving on the *Neville* on May 30, Doug was good-naturedly cautioned not to get comfortable because he would not be staying on board long. His repeatedly asked why, but his inquiries were met with the response "You'll know soon enough."[20]

Transport Division 17 remained in Wellington through late July. Despite the workload and the war, there was no way that Doug was going to miss out on the chance to enjoy Wellington. When liberty was announced, he was one of the first men off the ship. He reveled in his shore leave, allowing the people and culture of Wellington to lessen the tensions of war, if just for a few hours. As in every port, the gregarious Douglas Munro had no trouble forming new friendships, with both men and women. Making the most of his social and dance skills, Doug and Ray were regular patrons of the Majestic Cabaret, the premier dance hall on Willis Street. Featuring Laurie Paddi's orchestra, the cabaret was known for its lighting and large dance floor. Ray remembered that Doug made a lasting impression on one young lady who wrote to him on a regular basis during the followings months, as well as Doug's mother after the war.

"Soon enough," Doug did find out why he shouldn't get comfortable on the *Neville*. In mid-July, Doug, along with the transport division's command, was transferred to the USS *McCawley*, which had just arrived in Wellington. Ray was stationed on the *Hunter Liggett*. This marked the first time Doug and Ray had been separated since their enlistment.

The USS *McCawley* was an attack transport named after Charles G. McCawley, eighth commandant of the U.S. Marine Corps, who served from 1875 to 1891. The lead ship in its class, the *McCawley* was commissioned on September 11, 1940, with Captain H. D. McHenry in command. The *McCawley* also served as the flagship of Rear Admiral Richmond K. Turner, commander of the newly created Amphibious Force, South Pacific.

BORN IN PORTLAND, Oregon, on May 27, 1885, Richmond Kelly Turner was appointed to the Naval Academy and graduated with the Class of 1908. Having advanced through the ranks and serving in numerous billets and commands, Turner, then a captain, attended the Naval War College and served on that institution's staff from 1935 to 1938. In 1939, he was assigned to command the heavy cruiser *Astoria* during its diplomatic mission to Japan. Turner was the director of the Navy Department's War Plans Division in Washington, D.C., in 1940-41 and received the rank of rear admiral. He served as the assistant chief of staff to the commander in chief of the U.S. Fleet until June 1942, when he was appointed to take command of the Amphibious Force, South Pacific.

As JULY ENDED, the rains began. Normally, the monsoon season began in November. Midsummer was the time for the southeast trade winds, which generated little rain. That year, however, pelting rains fell continuously from New Zealand to Rabaul.

Always on the lookout for information, Ray said that he had heard rumors that the United States was planning its first major offensive of the war somewhere in the South Pacific, yet no one appeared to have any specifics. According to Ray, he and Doug swapped stories and information while ashore.

Ray said that while in port, they had few signalman responsibilities and spent most of their duty time with the Higgins boats. Doug, Ray and their Navy counterparts constantly inspected their boats, and even a hint of a problem, either structural or mechanical, was immediately addressed. Extra coats of paint were applied to the boats to combat the corrosive effects of the sea water. Coxswains made adaptations to make operation more efficient and effective. All these preparations hinted that something "big" was on the horizon. But no one seemed to know exactly what. If they did, no one was talking.

DURING THE WEEKS following the *Hunter Liggett's* arrival in port, numerous ships, including transports with thousands of men and equipment, destroyers, and cruisers, arrived daily. Ray said that neither he nor Doug could help but notice the increased number of small boats on each of the transports. While conducting amphibious exercises in both Onslow and Chesapeake Bays, each ship had fifteen to twenty boats. From what he could see now, each transport had taken on an additional ten to fifteen boats—some even more.

The continuous rains completely soaked the large stacks of supplies for the Marines. Cardboard boxes spilled their contents all over the docks. Cans, boxes, and other supplies rolled into the bay and created what appeared to be a large floating barge. Nearly six inches of mud brought trucks and ship-loading equipment to a near halt. Marines were left to load the cargo ships by hand.

Admiral Turner and General Vandegrift were notified that their mission was set to begin on August 1. Both commanders argued vehemently against that date and were able to delay the implementation of the plan until August 7, the date on which coastwatcher reports and reconnaissance flights indicated that the airfield on Guadalcanal would be complete. The primary concern of both commanders was supply. Logistically, the ships could only be loaded with items required for basic everyday survival and combat. Items such as sea bags, bedrolls, and tents were to be left behind, as were heavy equipment and motor transport. Bulk supplies of fuel, lubricants, and food rations were cut to sixty days. Ammunition was reduced to a ten-day supply from the scheduled fifteen.

While not privy to the details of the impending action, Doug and many of the other men believed that they were going to be involved in some major offensive and, from the cargo being loaded, were preparing to establish a forward operating base. Asking too many questions of their superiors was certainly not a good career move, but because of his rating as a signalman, coupled with his duties as a coxswain, Doug was often in a position to overhear snippets of conversations, which he was able to put together. But, for every piece of the puzzle that fit, there were several pieces missing. Could it be that even the divisional and Amphibious Force commanding officers did not know all of the operational details? Surely not.

Unknown to Doug or any of the tens of thousands of men assigned to Transport Division 17, security was so tight that Admiral Turner had not been briefed on his overall mission until he was under way for several days en route to New Zealand. Despite the secrecy, three islands in the Solomon chain received frequent mention: Tulagi, Florida, and Santa Cruz. As impressive as the numbers of assembled troops, transports, and warships were, Doug would soon learn that it was only one-third of the armada being assembled.

Early on the morning on July 22, with Rear Admiral Turner on board the flagship *McCawley*, the expeditionary force pulled away from its moorings in a single file. The twenty-two transports and their accompanying destroyers were joined by an escort of cruisers, including the USS *Astoria*, the USS *Quincy*, the USS *Vincennes*, and the USS *Chicago*, along with the Australian heavy cruisers *Canberra* and *Australia*, and headed north toward the Fiji Islands, where the entire Guadalcanal invasion fleet would rendezvous. Moving at only eleven knots, the column needed most of the day to sail beyond the range of covering aircraft from New Zealand.

Having meticulously checked and rechecked their boats, Doug and several of the coxswains were up on deck after evening chow when they noticed what appeared to be two carrier task forces approaching their position. It was announced over the ship's public address system that the approaching carrier task forces were that of the USS *Saratoga* and the USS *Wasp.*

As the announcement ended, everyone was ordered to destroy their diaries and journals, which unnerved everyone on board. No one said a word. Ray just looked around at the others, and wondered what they were about to experience. He worried about his friend Doug.[21]

When the USS *Enterprise* task force joined the armada the next day in the Coral Sea, the number of ships in the task force reached fifty. On board one of the transports was war correspondent Richard Tregaskis, who wrote, "We were conscious of the fact that this was one of the largest and strongest groups of war vessels ever gathered, certainly the largest and strongest of this war to date."[22] To put the size of the Guadalcanal invasion armada into perspective, the carrier task forces that conducted the attack on Wake Islands on December 23, 1941, had ten ships. The battle groups formed for the Doolittle raid conducted on April 18, 1942, on Tokyo and to repel the June 4–7, 1942, Japanese attack at Midway numbered two dozen ships each. With the invasion fleet observing radio silence, all communication was conducted by signalmen using flag signaling hoists and semaphores during the day and blinkers at night. Maintaining communication between the eighty ships during the four-day transit to Guadalcanal kept Doug and the other signalmen very busy. Doug and the other signalmen used alphabet flags, numeral pennants, numeral flags, and special flags and pennants for visual signaling. Messages were transmitted by hoisting a flag or a series of flags on a halyard. Each side of the ship had halyards and a "flag bag" that contained a full set of signal flags.

CHAPTER 5

OPERATION WATCHTOWER

Twelve days from their scheduled August 7 landing on Tulagi, Guadalcanal, and the nearby smaller islands of Florida, Gavutu, and Tanambogo, the Expeditionary Combined Task Force arrived in Fiji for a scheduled rehearsal. The combined task force consisted of Task Force 61 and Task Force 62. Task Force 61, under the command of Vice Admiral Frank Fletcher, was comprised of the carriers *Enterprise, Wasp,* and *Saratoga*; the battleship *North Carolina*; the cruisers *Minneapolis, Portland, San Francisco, Salt Lake City,* and *Atlanta*; and the destroyers *Balch, Gwin, Benham, Grayson, Lang, Sterrett, Aaron Ward, Laffey, Farenholt, Phelps, Farragut, Worden, MacDonough, Dale,* and *Morris*.

Task Force 62, under the command of Rear Admiral Richmond "Kelly" Turner, was made up of the cruisers *Chicago, Australia* (RAN), *Quincy, Astoria, Canberra* (RAN), *San Juan,* and *Hobart*

(RAN); the destroyers *Wilson, Jarvis, Blue, Ralph Talbot, Bagley, Patterson, Monssen, Buchanan, Helm, Henley, Ellet, Selfridge, Mugford,* and *Hull*; the minesweepers *Hopkins, Trever, Zane, Southard, Hovey,* and *Tracy*; and the transports *Little, McKean, Gregory, Calhoun, George F. Elliott, President Hayes, Fuller, President Jackson, Neville, Hunter Liggett, Heywood, Zelin, McCawley, Barnett, American Legion, President Adams, Crescent City, Bellatrix, Formalhaut, Athena, Betelgeuse, Libra,* and *Alchiba.* After the combined task force's arrival in Fiji, it was joined by the cruiser *Vincennes.*

The rehearsal exercise was a disappointment. Doug and his fellow coxswains could see that the coastline looked nothing as described in their operational briefings. With a lower than expected tide, the coral reefs loomed so ominously that the practice landing was canceled. Instead, Marines practiced descending cargo nets and boarding landing craft. Doug and other coxswains then circled the transports several times before the Marines reboarded their ships. As the Higgins boats were being reloaded on the ships, Doug continued to practice maneuvers—circling, simulating approaches, and throttling. He utilized every minute, and his boat was the last one off the water.[1] Cruisers practiced shore bombardment but consistently missed their targets. The aircraft target practice fared little better.

When not tending to the boats or practicing, and despite being attached to the Navy, Doug spent a lot of time with the Marines below deck. He felt more comfortable there.[2] Although not initially interested in the Marine Corps, he had grown to respect and admire the men known as "Devil Dogs," whose devotion to duty drove them to live like cattle in sweltering holds; sleep on tiered cots a few inches from the bunk above; shower in sea water; eat chow standing in mess halls slippery with water, sweat, and coffee; and wear the same uniform until it disintegrated, their socks so badly worn they resembled leggings, their boots contorted from constant exposure to sweat, sea water, and the sun. These were men who would eat that which would repulse others, men who would rather die than quit, men who always seemed to be the first to fight.

During the flawed rehearsal, senior commanders met on board the carrier *Saratoga*. Conducted by Vice Admiral Frank Fletcher, the meeting was attended by Rear Admiral Turner, commander of the amphibious force; Major General Alexander Vandegrift, commander of the landing force; Rear Admiral Leigh Noyes, Fletcher's chief of staff; Rear Admiral Thomas Kincaid, commander of the *Enterprise* task force; Rear Admiral John S. McCain, commander of land-based Navy aircraft in the area; and Rear Admiral Daniel Callaghan, Admiral Ghormley's chief of staff.[3] The importance of this meeting cannot be overstated. It was here that commanders were given their operational orders and the overall operational plan. The Watchtower commanders learned that upon approach to Savo Island, Task Force 62 would split into two squadrons. The squadrons were further divided into five groups.

Vice Admiral Fletcher, it turned out, neither had knowledge of nor interest in the Guadalcanal operation. Vandegrift wrote that Fletcher turned on Admiral Turner and angrily accused him of "instigating" the Solomons invasion. As Admiral Turner voiced his incredulous denial, Fletcher interrupted him and asked how long it would take to unload the troops. When Turner replied that he would need five days, Fletcher shook his head and said that two days would be sufficient.[4]

Vandegrift argued that five days of air cover from Fletcher's carriers were barely sufficient, and two days were suicidal. A protracted fist-pounding session ensued, and Fletcher declared that he would pull his carriers on the evening of the August 9, seventy-two hours after the operation commenced. The unspoken but well-known underlying issue that plagued the meeting was distrust of Fletcher's competency. It had been discussed at the most senior levels of the Navy that his promotion to vice admiral had been held up due to concerns about his command competency; his ace in the hole was his favor with Admiral Nimitz.[5]

Marine commanders were appalled at Fletcher's apparent lack of knowledge of amphibious landings in general as well as his stated disinterest in the operational landing plan. Both Turner and Vandegrift strenuously argued that his plan would leave the Marines and the landing craft unprotected. After the meeting, Admiral Turner verbally confronted Fletcher, even to the point of questioning his courage and resolve, all to no avail.[6] The senior commanders meeting as well as the rehearsal fell far short of expectations; both would prove prophetic.

Lieutenant Commander Dwight H. Dexter had been told by operational commanders that at some point early in the Guadalcanal landing he and a crew would be put ashore to establish a naval operating base, which would be known as Cactus. He would be the first Coast Guard officer ever placed in charge of a naval operating base and could handpick some of his men. When word got out, there were plenty of volunteers.[7]

Doug and the rest of the coxswains were given their rotational assignments in several briefings on July 31. Having the additional skills of a signalman, Doug was ordered to beach his boat after all the Marines were landed and attach himself to a Marine unit, where he would initiate ship-to-shore communication.[8]

THE SOLOMON ISLANDS AND GUADALCANAL

Extending about nine hundred miles in length, the Solomons were a wide-spread archipelago of mountainous, heavily forested volcanic islands and a few low-lying coral atolls running north to west, south of New Britain and New Ireland and northeast of New Guinea. There were six major islands and approximately a thousand smaller islands in the chain, ending in the Santa Cruz Islands of the far southeast.

Guadalcanal, the largest island in the Solomons chain, was located thirty-six hundred miles from Pearl Harbor. Covering an area of more than five thousand square miles, it was shaped like

Jamaica, but was only about half its size. Like most islands in the Pacific, it was of volcanic origin with a mountainous spine. Mount Austen, described in reconnaissance reports as the "Grassy Knoll," the tallest peak on the island, reached a height of more than eight thousand feet.

On the southern coast, the mountains fell steeply into the ocean, creating a natural barrier to movement. The northern coast was cut through with fast-moving rivers in the mountains that leveled off and mixed with the sea in still-water lagoons filled with saltwater crocodiles. A narrow beach guarded by palm and ironwood trees and covered with razor-sharp kunai grass stretched for miles overlooked by five-hundred-foot-high coral ridges. The tropical climate was insect ridden and rampant with mosquitoes carrying dengue, yellow fever, and malaria.

On Guadalcanal, Martin Clemens was frustrated. He had done everything asked of him—everything. He had kept Lieutenant Commander Feldt accurately informed about IJN activities on both Tulagi and Guadalcanal, right down to the number and description of every piece of equipment the IJN used. Other than the few bombs dropped in Tulagi harbor nearly two months before, nothing had been done about the Japanese presence on the island. Where were the Allied planes? By August 4, with their food stores completely depleted, Clemens and his men had to live on yams and pumpkins. The following day, his men reported that the Japanese had completed the airfield and planes could be expected in as little as two days. Clemens knew that if the airfield became operational, it would reduce the chances of driving the Japanese off the island to zero, which would further affect Allied operations in the region.

Due to operational security, he knew nothing of the American invasion plans. He also did not know that the planes he had been looking for had been flying over sixteen hundred miles of the South Pacific in search of enemy ships that could compromise the invasion force on its way to the Solomons.

The sixth of August brought a storm front that grounded both American and IJN planes. The IJN had planned to transfer sixty planes to its new airfield on Guadalcanal. The crews of the American planes based at Espíritu Santo in the New Hebrides worked more than twenty hours in the driving rain, forming a bucket brigade to hand-load twenty-five thousand gallons of fuel aboard the aircraft. The next day, regardless of weather, the planes would fly in support of the invasion. Clemens had not been forgotten, his information had not been ignored, and help was indeed on the way.

Throughout the sixth, the Marines and the boat crews on board the transport ships prepared for the battle to come. Sailors rigged booms to the heaviest of the landing craft to facilitate a quick launch. At various locations on board the ships, rations were distributed: concentrated coffee and biscuits, meat and beans, vegetable stew, and chocolate bars. Everyone received two to three days' supply—enough, it was believed, until field kitchens could be established ashore. On the artillery transports, the 75- and 105-millimeter howitzers were brought aloft and lashed to the gunwales; large coils of rope to tow them inland were strewn over the barrels.

On board his transport, Ray and the other coxswains tested their boats. He was sure that Doug was doing the same. The sputtering sound of dozens of landing-craft engines drowned out the noise of the other preparation activities. Ray later related:

> *As Doug stood at the throttle of his boat while it was unlashed and swung out on a davit, he saw Marines quietly sharpening knives and bayonets, inspecting canteens and grenades, blackening rifle sights, and applying oil to rifle bores. Machine gunners skillfully loaded 250-round ammunition belts in rectangular green cases. The Navy corpsmen assigned to the Marines checked medical and supply kits, loading extra medication and bandages in anticipation of the battle to come. As Doug watched, he realized*

his personal safety and that of his boat was secondary to the
mission of taking his Marines safely to the beaches, where
they would take the fight to the enemy. Much to his dismay,
he was scheduled for the third-wave assault on Tulagi. The
1st Marine Raider Battalion would be the first unit ashore.
He knew I was scheduled for the first wave on Guadalcanal
with the 5th Marine Regiment.[9]

As darkness fell, an announcement was heard throughout the ship: "Darken ship. The smoking lamp is out on all weather decks. All troops below decks." Some men headed for their holds far below the waterline. Others sought comfort in their religion. Still others wrote last letters home or lay on their bunks alone with their thoughts.[10]

After attending a brief Protestant service, Ray said that Doug mentally went over every conceivable scenario in mind. "That's just the kind of guy he was, ready for anything, and afraid of nothing." He was going to be responsible for transporting the Marines—the most important asset of the task force—safely to shore, then taking them critically needed supplies to keep them in the fight. He knew the Marines that would fill his boat, but just as important, the Marines knew Doug Munro.[11]

While both the Marines and Navy coxswains directed good-natured ribbing his way for his long hours of practice, they knew he was one of the best. His proficiency and willingness to help other coxswains did not escape the attention of Navy commanders. Ray commented with a chuckle that questions about small-boat maneuverability and handling frequently received the response "Go ask Munro."[12]

THE OPPOSING FORCES

As the Allies would soon learn, the Japanese were highly mobile and excellent at camouflage. They were tenacious and subscribed to the code of Bushido; they preferred death to capture and were used to harsh discipline and lack of comforts and necessities of life. The Imperial Japanese Army was well organized up to the regimental level, but rarely operated at the division level. Its weakness was overestimating its own capabilities while underestimating that of its opponent. The Imperial Japanese Navy was a highly efficient organization that could operate effectively either day or night, was highly disciplined, and skillfully utilized its personnel and equipment. Its weakness was its failure to exploit its tactical successes, unable to turn them into strategic victories.[13]

The American forces consisted of the newly created 1st Marine Division, which was made up of noncombat volunteers using World War I–vintage equipment; the unit also had insufficient medical supplies, communications, and logistics to effectively manage a prolonged campaign at the end of the American supply line. The American artillery was highly accurate and could deliver large volumes of high-angle fire either offensively or defensively. The Americans also used their M3A1 (Stuart) light tanks effectively and quickly learned valuable lessons in jungle warfare.[14]

THE MARINES

Vandegrift planned to use approximately fifteen thousand men, with five thousand in reserve, organized into combat groups. Combat Group A, under the command of Colonel LeRoy P. Hunt, was ordered to land on Guadalcanal's Beach Red, about halfway between Lunga and Koli Points on the north coast of the island, and seize the beachhead. Combat Group B, under the command of Colonel Clifton B. Cates, was ordered to land at Beach Red fifty minutes after Combat Group A, pass through its right, and seize the "grassy knoll" about four miles south of Lunga Point.[15]

The Tulagi Group, under the command of Lieutenant Colonel Merritt A. Edson, was ordered to land on Beach Blue, on the southwest coast, and seize the northwest section of the island. The Gavutu Group, under the command of Major Robert H. Williams, was ordered to land on the east coast of Gavutu island four hours later, seize the island, later pressing on to Tanambogo. The Florida Group, under the command of Major Robert E. Hill, was ordered to land on Florida Island near Halavo thirty minutes after the Tulagi Group and seize the village. The remaining groups were held in reserve and would deploy when given orders.[16] Shore party commanders would be responsible for controlling traffic in beach areas, and for calling troop commanders in their immediate vicinity for assistance in getting supplies from the beaches to supply dumps inland.

THE APPROACH

As the armada of ships approached the Solomons at a speed of about seven knots, Task Force Negat, several miles head, maintained a generally parallel course and provided reconnaissance and patrols. Task Force Tare had assumed a circular formation, with the transports and cargo ships proceeding in five columns in the center. The *Hunter Liggett*, the first ship in the middle column, acted as the guide for the formation. The screen was made up of three concentric circles around the *Hunter Liggett*, the first circle one mile from the ship, the second a radius of two miles, and the third a radius of three miles.[17]

As the expeditionary force continued its voyage, beginning on August 1, and continuing for the next five days, Allied planes bombed Japanese bases near Tulagi and Lunga Point. Patrol bombers conducted extensive searches of the operations area.[18]

Just after 0130, watch officers on board the ships of the invasion fleet saw the dark outline of Guadalcanal, broad on the starboard bow, under a quarter moon. Marines lined the starboard rail and pointed their field glasses toward the target. Several minutes later, Savo Island, a five-mile-long by two-mile-wide strip of land located just northeast of the northern tip of Guadalcanal, came into view. At 0300, as scheduled, the two squadrons separated. Squadron Yoke passed north of Savo Island toward Tulagi, code-named Ringbolt, while Squadron XRay passed to the east and south of Savo Island toward Guadalcanal, code-named Cactus. Neither squadron was challenged by Japanese forces, despite passing within six thousand yards of Lunga Point, the location of known artillery batteries.[19]

One hundred miles to the south, the carriers *Saratoga*, *Enterprise*, and *Wasp* turned slowly into the wind, their Dauntlesses, Avengers, and Wildcats waiting on deck. Just before dawn, all aircraft launched, with forty-four headed for targets on Guadalcanal, forty-one targeted for Tulagi, and seven to bomb enemy targets on the eastern end of Florida Island and Malaita.

Forty-five minutes later, the cruiser *Quincy* began shelling enemy shore positions. As the first shell was fired, Martin Clemens and his men ran toward the beach, yelling with joy. Thirty minutes later, the transports swung bow-in toward Guadalcanal and stopped nine thousand yards off Red Beach. Cruisers and destroyers not providing artillery support formed a double arc around the transports as protection against submarine and air attack.

RINGBOLT

Lieutenant Colonel Merritt Edson and his Raiders were the first ashore, hitting Tulagi's south coast and moving inland toward a ridge that ran the length of the island. Blue Beach was not the best beach on the island, which was its merit. Major Justice Chambers recalled that it "was probably the last place the Japs thought we would land. It was completely surrounded by coral reefs, and this made it necessary to halt the boats on the edge of the reef. Then everybody had to plunge into the water and wade to shore. This is no fun, as we had found out during our training in Samoa, because coral reefs are dotted with holes and at any moment you are likely to step into water that is over your head. The best beach on Tulagi was at the other end of the island and the Japanese had clearly expected that any hostile landing would be made there. So they had very lightly fortified the beach where we landed."[20]

The first two waves of Marines ashore encountered pockets of stiff enemy resistance in the undergrowth of the island's jungle vegetation. Commanders had anticipated strong resistance on Guadalcanal, according to intelligence report estimates of the enemy's strength; however, based on those reports, they did not anticipate the resistance encountered on Tulagi.

When the third wave was called for, Doug joined his two crewmen on his Higgins boat. After fixing an American flag to the stern, he stood at the throttle as his boat lowered to the clanging of the davits. Upon reaching the water, he started the engine and maintained his boat alongside the transport. He heard the constant sound of mortar, automatic-weapons, and artillery fire coming from Tulagi, where his Marines were taking it to the Japanese. He heard the sound and felt the percussion made by the large deck guns of the ships as they pounded away at the beaches and inland targets. Doug could see the bright colors of the explosions where the bombs landed. As the planes dove in, they strafed the beaches and pounded every building that could shelter the enemy. Heavy smoke clouds filled the air. The deep gurgling sound of the diesel engines of his boat were muffled as the ocean swells lapped against it. Everyone was tense.[21]

Marines began moving down the nets like four-legged crabs, hanging on to the ropes with clenched fists as the movement of the ship banged them mercilessly against the steel hull, their helmets bumping over their eyes. Each man carried bandoliers that crisscrossed their chests and cartridge belts packed with bullets. Some carried mortars and machine-gun components; others held automatic weapons. Reaching the bottom of the net, the men jumped the remaining six feet and, with the help of the two crewmen, scrambled to sitting positions, their heads below the gunwales. After the last man was on board and seated, and the men had fixed bayonets to their weapons, Doug taxied slowly away and joined three other boats from the transport as they took their place in the landing circle.[22]

As the third wave approached the beach, no Japanese resistance was encountered. The moment his boat grated to a halt on the coral shoals, Doug dropped the ramp. Several Marines climbed over the port and starboard sides while others ran out the front, splitting in all directions. Several of the Marines struggled with their heavy loads in the waist-deep water and went under, but they were quickly yanked to the surface by their buddies, their hands and knees torn and bloodied by the razor-sharp coral. Within seconds, all of the troops had disembarked. Doug raised the ramp and backed away from the beach until he was able to turn around and proceed to the transport for another load of Marines.

After two runs, the third wave was on the beach. The Marines moved quickly. After the boat crews safely delivered all of the Marines ashore, Doug beached and secured his boat, grabbed the semaphore flags and blinker light, and assumed his signalman duties. He teamed up with a platoon of Marines he knew as they made their way inland.[23]

Throughout the day and into the evening, using flag semaphore, Doug relayed details about the Marines' progress to the ships offshore.[24] Despite the early resistance, the sheer number of Marines coming ashore overpowered the defending Japanese, who moved further inland. By nightfall, the Raiders had reached the former British residency that overlooked the harbor and dug in for the night.

Because of Japanese resistance inland, the Marines were unable to secure the entire island before nightfall. During the night, the Japanese launched several counterattacks in an effort to drive the Marines back to the beach. Doug, along with several Marines, had moved into a densely covered area. Unable to see more than a few feet ahead, the Marines fired short bursts into the dense foliage every few minutes as a precaution against the frequent Japanese charges. Doug had looked for a suitable location to send messages, but he was unsuccessful. The Marines had repeatedly instructed Doug to remain low, but he ignored them and climbed up on a large exposed rock outcropping, from which he sent messages with his blinker throughout the night. To protect him, the Marines crawled up on the rock and continued their intermittent firing as a precaution. At daybreak, Doug and the Marines bristled as they found several dead Japanese troops within yards of their location. Doug looked at the Marines, smiled, and nodded. The Marines just shook their heads as one inquired, "Are you sure you're not one of us?"[25]

Japanese troops had taken up positions on the reverse slopes, which gave them better visibility against the crests and sky, and permitted intense surprise fire of devastating effect at short ranges. However, when they counterattacked out of these positions, they suffered so many casualties that they did not have men enough to hold their ground the next day.

Doug and his crew loaded their boat with several of the first day's casualties. The Raiders had lost ninety-nine men, while the 2nd Battalion had lost fifty-six. Doug had known several of the men on his boat. Saddened, he knew there would be more. After the casualties had been taken on board the transports, Doug and his crew transported supplies and equipment ashore.[26]

CHAPTER 6

NAVAL OPERATING BASE CACTUS

The main body of about ten thousand Marines hit the middle of Guadalcanal's northern coast just after 0900 on the morning of August 7. Despite the warnings from the boat commanders, Ray saw no signs of opposition awaiting them.[1] As the boats scraped the sandy bottom and came to a stop, two battalions of the 5th Marines climbed over the sides of the landing craft into knee-to-waist-deep water and fanned out along a front of about two thousand yards to provide cover for the 1st Marines, coming in behind them. The 5th Marines turned west and made its way to the village of Kukum, while the 1st Marines proceeded south toward Mount Austen, also referred to as the Grassy Knoll. Ground commanders had been told that the Grassy Knoll would be two miles inland across relatively easy terrain. In fact, it was four miles through dense jungle.

Marines, who had become somewhat soft during the weeks on board ship, struggled as they scrambled up thick muddy hills and slid down the other side, gasping for breath in the humid heat, crossing fields of razor-sharp kunai grass and what appeared to be a series of rivers that were, in fact, two rivers that doubled back. With no scouts or flankers probing the dense jungle, they would have been easy targets for any Japanese troops waiting in ambush. There were none. The Japanese Special Naval Landing Force, along with about seventeen hundred native laborers, had fled west of the Lunga River into the path of the 5th Marines.[2]

In the jungle, hindered by torrential rains and mosquitoes and the terrain, the Marines slowly moved toward their objectives. As they advanced, they began to get a glimpse of their environment. Clemens described Guadalcanal in James Brady's *Hero of the Pacific*:

> *She was a poisonous morass. Crocodiles in her creeks or patrolled her turgid backwaters. Her jungles were alive with slithering, crawling, scuttling things; with giant lizards that barked like dogs, with huge, red furry spiders, with centipedes and leeches and scorpions, with rats and bats and fiddler crabs and one big species of land-crab which moved through the bush with all the stealth of a steamroller . . . there were also devouring myriads of sucking, biting, burrowing insects that found sustenance in human blood; armies of fiery white ants . . . swarms upon swarms of filthy black flies that fed upon open cuts and made festering ulcers of them, and clouds of malaria-bearing mosquitos.[3]*

Years later, author Richard Frank's description still paints a vivid image:

> *The lords of Guadalcanal's jungle were the great hardwood trees that soared up to 150 feet and had girths as much as 40 feet across. Their straight trunks sprouted only high branches that formed a 'sunproof roof.' Their massive flared*

roots snaked across the surface like thick trip wires while other leafy vines festooned the trunks of the jungle floor . . . Sheltered in the dark bramble were wild dogs, pigs, lizards, and gigantic bush rats the size of rabbits. Fish filled the streams and crocodiles slithered in and out of watercourses and mangrove swamps near the shore. . . . The sour odor of decay permeated the steamy stagnant air, for beneath the lushness omnipresent rot made the yellow clay earth porous.[4]

On the beach, Ray and more than a hundred other boat crews brought in supplies, equipment, and rations.[5] At midnight, the 1st Marines, ordered to forgo the Grassy Knoll, proceeded to the airfield from the south. Arriving just after dawn at the newly named Henderson Field, the Marines discovered a cache of antiaircraft batteries, ammunition dumps, a complex of wharves, bridges, ice plants, radio receiver stations, power and oxygen plants, more than a hundred Chevy two-ton trucks, road rollers, and fifty to sixty thousand gallons of gasoline stored in underground pipes.[6]

Back on the beach, with only a few hundred men delegated to stevedore duty, the scene soon became chaotic as supplies were dumped ashore by hundreds of boats. The confusion multiplied as untrained coxswains took rations to beaches marked for fuel and medical supplies were mixed in with ammunition.

Delayed by a late-morning air raid by Japanese planes, Lieutenant Commander Dwight H. Dexter, USCG, went ashore in the early afternoon of August 8 to establish and command Naval Operating Base Cactus. In 1942, Dexter was already a twenty-year veteran of the Coast Guard. The son of Dr. Edwin Dexter, who served in a variety of governmental diplomatic posts in Central America and Europe, Dwight moved to various posts with his parents until he received an appointment to the Coast Guard Academy in 1922.

He returned to civilian life after two years before reentering the service as an ensign in 1926. For the next fifteen years, he served on the East Coast and in the Caribbean on board the Coast Guard–manned prohibition-enforcement destroyer, the USS *Patterson*, and the cutters *Champlain* and *Marion*. After sea duty, he served five years with the Coast Guard Rifle and Pistol Team, three as commander. In early 1941, as war loomed ever closer, Dexter received a billet on the staff of the commander of Transport Division 3. Immediately after Pearl Harbor, he transferred to the staff of the commander of Transport Group, South Pacific.

NOB Cactus's primary mission was to run supplies and troops from the transports to the beaches of Guadalcanal. Arriving ashore with about a hundred handpicked Coast Guard and Navy personnel from various ships, including Ray Evans, Dexter set up headquarters in the former manager's house on the Lever Brothers coconut plantation inside the Marine defensive perimeter at the village of Lunga, just east of Lunga Point. The simple white house was in good condition despite the heavy naval bombardment the previous day. Men were assigned to quickly build a critically needed tool shed for the maintenance and repair of the landing craft and what little machinery was available. A communications signal tower was also constructed, from coconut logs.

Dexter saw the mass confusion on the beaches as landing craft brought ashore supplies to reinforce the Marines. Upon his arrival, the beaches were stacked so high that cartons were toppling into the water, and there was little cooperation or coordination in getting the supplies off the beach and moved forward to the various supply dumps. The beach itself had become a dumpsite.

Cactus was the only NOB ever commander by a Coast Guard officer; as such, some Marines assigned to assist with moving supplies refused to take orders from Coast Guardsmen or assist with the cargo, saying that they were fighting men, not longshoremen. Anyone found to be insubordinate was relieved of duty and transferred back to his ship; there they faced disciplinary action from their commanders. Ray recalled with a chuckle, "I don't remember any Coast Guard men being insubordinate. To tell you the truth, I don't think any of them were stupid enough to cross Dexter. The Marines sure found that out soon enough."[7]

Seeing that supplies were being ruined by sea water, Dexter climbed atop a stack of cartons and began directing the unloading and transfer efforts. He had Ray and other Coast Guardsmen organize the transfer of supplies from the beach to the village of Kukum and Lunga Point within the perimeter.[8]

At noon, Japanese bombers targeted the ships in the channel, dropping their bombs from twenty thousand feet to avoid American antiaircraft fire. While most of their bombs fell harmlessly into the channel, several ships were hit and damaged. The destroyer USS *Jarvis* was torpedoed by Japanese planes but managed to get away under its own power. The following day, the ship was again attacked by Japanese planes; this time, it was sunk. None of the 233-man crew survived. The USS *George F. Elliott* was set ablaze by a Japanese plane that crashed into the aft superstructure. Efforts to control the fires were unsuccessful and the ship was abandoned. The crew was rescued by the *Hunter Liggett*.

About an hour later, twenty to twenty-five high-level twin-engine Japanese bombers came in over Savo Island and headed for the transports, which sent the Marines and the boat crews scattering for cover. Three of the attacking planes were knocked down by the screening ships and transports. The remaining enemy aircraft executed a pattern bombing run but failed to hit any of their intended targets. As the planes disappeared behind the island's mountains, Ray and the other boat crews resumed bringing men, supplies, and equipment ashore.[9] An hour later, seven to ten single-engine Japanese dive-bombers came in over Tulagi and initiated a bombing run. After three misses, one bomb hit the destroyer *Mugford*, resulting in eight killed, seventeen wounded, and ten missing, but the ship survived. U.S. fighters from the three carriers constantly engaged enemy aircraft throughout the afternoon.

Despite the Japanese air attacks, Ray and his fellow Coast Guard and Navy coxswains landed about eleven thousand Marines. Facing the Fletcher deadline of August 9, boat crews work at a frenzied pace bringing in cargo from the transports.

Dripping with sweat after hours working in the sun, Evans and Dexter walked to chow. As the men ate, Dexter inquired, "Where's Munro, anyway?" Ray began to explain that Doug had been assigned to Tulagi. Dexter interrupted him, growling, "I don't care about all that. I need him here. They are mopping up over there. Get him over here!" Without finishing his meal, Ray exited the house and sent for his friend.[10]

That evening, operation commanders met on board the *McCawley*. Admiral Turner informed General Vandegrift that Admiral Fletcher was pulling his ships out early. Before dusk, prior to sending a message to Admiral Ghormley requesting approval to withdraw, Fletcher had turned his ships southward, taking three aircraft carriers, one battleship, six heavy cruisers, and sixteen destroyers—essentially the major portion of the invasion fleet's strength—out of the fight. Later, in his radio message to Admiral Ghormley, Fletcher claimed, "Fighter-plane strength reduced from ninety-nine to seventy-eight. In view of the large number of enemy torpedo planes and bombers in this area, I recommend the immediate withdrawal of my carriers. Request tankers be sent forward immediately as fuel running low."[11] The fact that his carrier task force had not been spotted by the enemy, that his fighter strength was double the enemy's, and that his bunkers contained enough fuel to keep him in the area for at least two more days was irrelevant to the expedition's commander, who had committed to both Admiral Turner and General Vandegrift that they would have air support for seventy-two hours. Admiral Fletcher retreated. Admiral Turner had a colorful description for Fletcher's retreat: "He's left us bare ass!"[12]

Concerned about his men, Vandegrift went across to Tulagi to see how many supplies had been brought ashore. He knew Guadalcanal received less than half of its sixty-day ration; it was certain that with all the fighting, Tulagi had less.[13]

In the early morning hours of the ninth, the men on Tulagi and Guadalcanal watched as the Battle of Savo Island unfolded. During the thirty-two-minute battle, the Japanese navy sunk four

The former Munro home in Cle Elum, Washington, circa 2011. (Gary Williams)

James Munro. (Courtesy of the Sheehan family)

Edith Munro. (Courtesy of the Sheehan family)

Douglas and Patricia Munro. (Courtesy of the Sheehan family)

Douglas Munro as a member of the Sons of the American Legion drum and bugle corps. (Courtesy of the Sheehan family)

The Cle Elum substation, operated by James Munro, located next to the Munro home. (Gary Williams)

Douglas and Patricia Munro enjoy the bountiful snow in the Cascades. (Courtesy of the Sheehan family)

Douglas, Patricia, and "Charlie" find skiing a more enjoyable mode of travel. (Courtesy of the Sheehan family)

Douglas Munro Coast Guard enlistment photograph. (Courtesy of the Sheehan family)

Raymond J. Evans enlistment photograph. (Courtesy of the Sheehan family)

Douglas Munro Coast Guard portrait, circa 1940. (Courtesy of the Sheehan family)

Douglas Munro civilian portrait taken in New York City, circa 1940. (Courtesy of the Sheehan family)

Douglas Munro on duty on board the CGC *Spencer*. (Courtesy of the Sheehan family)

The CGC *Spencer* with newly applied battle paint. (Courtesy of the U.S. Coast Guard)

Douglas Munro ascends the superstructure on board the CGC *Spencer*. (Courtesy of the Sheehan family)

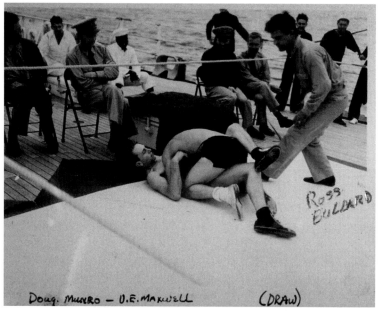

Douglas "Bunting Tosser" Munro participates in a wrestling match on board the CGC *Spencer*. (Courtesy of the Sheehan family)

Patricia (Munro) Sheehan with her children, Christopher and Douglas. (Courtesy of the Sheehan family)

Dwight H. Dexter, then a captain. (Courtesy of the Sheehan family)

Landing craft prepare to board Marines bound for the beaches of Guadalcanal. (Courtesy of the U.S. Coast Guard)

The Marines go ashore on Guadalcanal. (Courtesy of the U.S. Coast Guard)

Landing craft used by Coast Guardsmen during World War II. (Courtesy of the U.S. Coast Guard)

Supplies and equipment go ashore following the Marine landing on Guadalcanal. (Courtesy of the U.S. Coast Guard)

Allied heavy cruisers: the HMAS *Canberra*, the USS *Astoria*, the USS *Quincy*, and the USS *Vincennes*. The destroyers USS *Ralph Talbot*, USS *Bagley*, and USS *Patterson* were heavily damaged.[14]

At the morning light, the transports dispatched their entire contingent of small boats to look for survivors. As they approached, they found more than a thousand oil-covered sailors, many badly burned or seriously wounded, hanging on to empty shell casings, life rafts, crates, and anything else that would keep their heads above water. Trails of blood had thickened the water and attracted sharks that savagely fed on human remains. Marines on the ships and boat crew members killed more than a dozen sharks with rifles. Munro's boat joined those from other transports entering the billowing clouds of burning fuel that rose from the surface. The boat crews began to pull the cold, exhausted, and badly burned and injured Marines and sailors from the shark-infested waters. Despite their best efforts, some wounded men disappeared with appalling suddenness, a few screaming, others silently. Within five hours, more than seven hundred survivors, many badly burned or injured, had been pulled on board the boats and transported to the transport ships; the others were gone. American losses reached twelve hundred. The Australian ship *Canberra* lost more than eighty men, all resting at the sandy ocean floor of what would be called Iron Bottom Sound.[15]

Ray related that when Doug returned to the transport ship, an officer leaned over the gunwale and yelled, "Munro, you've been transferred. Get yourself and your boat over to Cactus and report to Dexter." The two Navy crewmen assigned to his boat scurried up the cargo nets. Leaving his sea bag on board the transport, Doug circled his boat around and began the twenty-mile trek across the channel.[16]

As he slowed for his approach to the beach, he saw Ray standing with his hands on his hips, a big grin on his face. Dexter stood next to Ray, arms folded across his chest. As the bowline was secured, Doug climbed out of his boat wearing only a hat, khaki shorts, and boots and carrying his rifle. Ray confided, "I think Dexter was trying to keep from laughing. He said, 'Is that how you report for duty, son?'" With a big smile on his face, Doug simply replied as he gave a halfhearted salute, "It is today, sir!" Dexter looked down and just shook his head and said, "Both of you, get yourselves some chow, we got work to do." As Doug and Ray turned away, Dexter said, "Munro, get a shirt on . . . before chow."[17]

Their first stop was Ray's little bunk area, located at the base of the newly constructed signal tower next to NOB headquarters. There, he tossed Doug one of his faded blue long-sleeved shirts, which left him with three, including the one he was wearing. Before morning, each would have two.

Doug buttoned his shirt and rolled up both sleeves several turns as they headed toward the mess tent. Ray looked over at Doug and said, "You'd better not let Dexter see your shirttail out. I'd tuck that in if I were you." While they walked, Doug tucked his shirt in and Ray gave him a quick overview of the beach operations: "What a mess," Doug said. Ray laughed and replied, "You should have seen it when we got here. Dexter sent quite a few men packing." As they entered the mess tent, Ray added, "I'm glad you're here. I can use all the help I can get. Besides, you're better with the boats. Lord knows, we can use that."[18]

After chow, Ray showed Doug the location of the closest bomb shelters. Then the two men assisted with supply and cargo unloading until well into the evening.[19]

ON AUGUST 9, the top naval commanders were faced with the sheer magnitude of the previous night's losses and the undeniable fact that "the Expeditionary Force Commander [Admiral Fletcher] had displayed a monumental lack of judgment, to say the least."[20] Due to Fletcher's retreat, Turner felt he had no choice but to withdraw his unprotected transports and cargo ships back to New Guinea. Turner informed Vandegrift of his decision early that morning. The general immediately called a conference of his staff and regimental commanders as well as Lieutenant Commander Dexter. He informed them of the actions taken by Fletcher and Turner. After several officers vented their anger and frustration, Vandegrift spoke softly and bluntly. He said that the Navy was leaving and no one knew if or when it would return. As a result, the remaining forces would be open to every form of attack: by land, from the air, and from the sea. He ordered his commanders to inform every man in his unit that they had been abandoned, but also instructed them to tell the men that Guadalcanal would not become another Bataan.[21]

The meeting was turned over to Vandegrift's operations officer, who provided their four-pronged operational directives going forward. They were

> *to hold a perimeter roughly 7,500 yards wide from west to east and penetrating inland about 3,500 yards. It would be bounded on its eastern or right flank by the Tenaru River and on the west or left by the Kukum Hills. Its northern or seaward front would be the most heavily fortified, because it was here that Vandegrift expected the Japanese to counterattack. Its landward rear would be the most lightly defended, for here the terrain was jungle and jumbled hills and could held by outposts tied together by roving patrols. The First Marines were to hold the Tenaru and the beach line west to the Lunga River. The Fifth Marines would hold the beach from the Lunga west to Kukum and around back to the Lunga. The Eleventh Marines would set up 75-mm and 105-mm howitzers in central positions from which to strike any point on the line. The 90-mm anti-aircraft guns of the Third Defense Battalion were to emplace northwest of Henderson Field, and the 75-mm half-tracks were to dig in north of the airfield and to be ready for movement to prepared positions on the beach. Vandegrift would hold his tank company and one battalion from the First Marines in reserve.[22]*

At noon, all offshore ships called in and hoisted their boats. By late afternoon, the last ships had disappeared eastward through the channel. The Coast Guard and the Marines were on their own. On both Tulagi and Guadalcanal, General Vandegrift ordered rations reduced to two meals per day, a reduction that remained in effect for six weeks. Work groups were assigned to accomplish the four directives. To complicate their efforts, only eighteen spools of barbed wire had been brought ashore. The ships had left with all squad, platoon, and company tools—axes, saws, post-hole diggers, shovels, spades, and picks—as well as antitank and antipersonnel mines.[23]

There was some good news: The Marines had completed their inventory of captured equipment at the airfield, which included four heavy tractors, six road rollers, and two gas-powered locomotives with hopper cars. Luckily, one critical piece of equipment had made it ashore—a medium bulldozer. This allowed the men to move quickly on airfield preparation.

Also in the cargo holds of the ships heading south were search radars, ground-to-air radio equipment, air-raid sirens, and surveying and mapping equipment. However, the Marines discovered that the Japanese had constructed an effective air-raid warning system and found an assortment of high-quality drafting instruments at the airfield. In between Japanese air attacks, Doug, Ray, and a large contingent of men moved supplies and dug foxholes, while others patrolled. Earlier in the day, Marines had consolidated positions ashore and seized the airfield, which was immediately named Henderson Field, in honor of Major Lofton Henderson, USMC, the commander of Squadron VMSB-241 and the first Marine Corps aviator killed in the Battle of Midway.

By August 12, the Marines had established their beachhead with a perimeter approximately seven miles long and two miles deep, and the runway at Henderson Field extended almost twenty-six hundred feet. That evening, a patrol of twenty-five Marines under the command of Colonel Frank Goettge, a Marine intelligence officer, was sent to reconnoiter the entrenched Japanese west of the Matanikau, a fast-moving river located just over a mile west of Kukum, which had become the line of demarcation between the opposing forces, with the Marines to the east and the IJA to the west. During this action, Goettge was killed, along with nineteen of his Marines. The survivors described their reactions to the unspeakable atrocities inflicted on those killed: "That day on the Matanikau we beheld all the horrors of war, all the degrees of degradation to which the human race could descend. . . . What kind of warfare was this? The Articles of War seemed to ring hollow. . . . It's hard to overestimate the speed and depth at which a story such as this travels among the enlisted."[24]

By evening, a thin beach defense that extended from the Ilu River to the west around Lunga to about a thousand yards west and south of the village of Kukum was established and reinforced with dug in 37-mm and .50-caliber guns stationed to hinder the Japanese landing that General Vandegrift was convinced was on its way.

Fearing attacks by Japanese submarines, for the next ten nights, NOB Cactus boats conducted antisubmarine patrols of the waters off Guadalcanal. Ray described the patrols: "Those sub patrols went on for about ten days or so. No subs or activity was ever noticed until this night. About one in the morning a minisub suddenly surfaced close aboard and turned his light on us, then immediately doused the light and submerged. I hollered at my coxswain to run toward the sub in the direction it was pointed and we would loosen the depth charges. Instead, he turned away and gunned us full speed the other way. What a disappointment, our only chance to get a sub by LCP gone forever."[25]

The next morning before dawn, Doug was up and making modifications to their quarters. Within several days, they had become the envy of both the Marines and their fellow Coast Guardsmen. Their quarters had a floor, two windows, a door, and a canvas roof. Although their quarters were lavish compared to the foxholes many of the Marines occupied, Doug and Ray spent little time there.[26] Work was frequently halted by Japanese air raids, which often resulted in boat trips to pick up downed pilots, wounded soldiers from the ships who were to be airlifted to hospitals, or survivors from ships hit by bombs.

On August 15, the destroyer-transports *Little*, *McKean*, and *Gregory* arrived with a Marine air operations detachment, along with four hundred drums of aviation gasoline, nearly three hundred bombs, belted aircraft ammunition, tools, and spare parts. That same evening, however, the Japanese landed supplies on western Guadalcanal, plus two hundred reinforcements. By the end of August, the U.S. air contingent on Guadalcanal comprised a total of eighty-six pilots and sixty-four planes, but General Vandegrift knew that the Japanese were reinforcing their positions at a much quicker rate, not only with supplies, but fresh troops who both outnumbered and outgunned the Americans.

In a period of three weeks, most of the Marines had become emaciated from their twice-daily ration of rice and the ever-increasing workload by day and patrolling by night. Many were ravaged by dysentery or eaten by rot, and the rate of malaria victims was rising dramatically. For every man lost in combat, five were lost to disease.

At NOB Cactus, Ray recalled, "You could see that Doug was pretty much was in charge of our contingent of small boats and tank lighters. Officers, including Dexter himself, would consult with him on questions regarding small-boat missions, maintenance, and things like that. In addition to his ability to handle the boats, he had emerged as a leader. Everyone could see that, plus what he did on Tulagi followed him to Guadalcanal. The Marines thought he was great and so did I."[27]

As August turned to September, many of the Coast Guardsmen, including Doug and Ray, began nighttime reconnaissance of the enemy. Rigged with depth charges, they volunteered for forward missions taking Marines to remote locations to probe for Japanese troops, built and manned machine-gun nests, and assisted in the construction of bunkers and shelters.

The twenty-hour workdays, the restricted rations, and the environment took their toll on both Doug and Ray. Both had contracted malaria, but because of the heat, humidity, stress, and long days, neither thought about their illness. They believed that the fever, sweating, cough, malaise, and nausea they were experiencing were just part of working on a tropical island. Both were given Atabrine. However, there was only a limited supply of the drug on the island.[28] When the Japanese captured the Dutch East Indies, they also captured more than 90 percent of the world's supply of cinchona bark, which was used to make both Atabrine and quinine. Because of the shortage, American forces on Guadalcanal suffered numerous recurrences of the disease. Doug's previous bout with pneumonia only exacerbated his malarial symptoms.

The USS *Betelgeuse* arrived at Lunga Point on September 1 with companies A and D of the 6th Naval Construction Battalion. The Seabees, as men in the naval construction battalions were known, set up a base of operations at Henderson Field, taking over construction and maintenance responsibilities from the Marines. While the Marine engineers had completed the work to make the field usable for fighters, the wide, flat surface provided little to no drainage. With the near-daily pelting rains, the heavy plane traffic tore up and rutted the runway's surface. The Seabees inherited the dual task of keeping the airfield in continuous usable condition and extending the runway from three thousand to five thousand feet to accommodate B-17s and B-24s.

Marines responsible for protecting Henderson Field dug diagonal trenches and foxholes along a thousand-foot line and also received a significant resupply of munitions in preparation for the fight they knew was coming. The fight came on September 12–14 in what has been called the Battle of Edson's Ridge, in honor of then Lieutenant Colonel Merritt Edson, who led the Marine forces in the battle. Here, the Japanese encountered a historic defeat that proved to be a turning point in the Pacific War. The battle was the only time during the land campaign when the Marines could have been so soundly defeated that Japanese forces could have retaken Henderson Field. But the Marines held.

Vice Admiral Turner had conferred on Guadalcanal with operational commanders on September 12 and informed them of Admiral Ghormley's assessment and decision that he could no longer support the Marines on the island. Turner, however, was convinced that the Guadalcanal campaign could be won in light of Vandegrift's order to bring the 3rd Battalion, 2nd Marines from Tulagi to Guadalcanal.

September 18 was a red-letter day for the men on Guadalcanal. Early in the morning that day, the newly formed Task Force 65, consisting of three cruisers plus destroyers and minesweepers, anchored off Kukum. Six Navy planes arrived at Henderson Field. More than four thousand fresh, fully equipped Marines arrived off Lunga Point on board six transports, accompanied by the destroyers *Monssen* and *MacDonough*. Among the Marine reinforcements was the 1st Battalion, 7th Marines of the 1st Marine Division, including Lieutenant Colonel Lewis B. "Chesty" Puller and Gunnery Sergeant John Basilone. By the time he landed on Guadalcanal, Puller was already a living Marine legend, having received two Navy Crosses. Basilone would receive a second chance at life and soon become a Marine Corps legend in his own right.

Word had been received regarding the threat of a Japanese air raid, and NOB Cactus boat crews worked tirelessly to ensure a rapid unloading of the amphibious ships so they could sail out of the channel, where they were vulnerable to attack.[29] Meanwhile, the *Monssen* and the *MacDonough* heavily shelled Japanese positions on the island. Marine commanders, including Puller, remembered the debacle that followed Admiral Fletcher's withdrawal of the invasion support fleet; to ensure that it did not reoccur, Puller personally supervised the job of unloading. When the ships departed early that evening, all of them were nearly empty.

Three transports not part of Task Force 65 arrived with an emergency shipment of aviation gasoline. The boats of NOB Cactus, along with those from the transports, put ashore 3,823 drums of fuel, 147 vehicles, 1,012 tons of rations, the 7th Marines' engineering equipment, and ammunition, consisting of ten units of fire with hand grenades and 81-millimeter mortar shells. The ammunition resupply was the first since the landing.[30]

The importance of the arrival of the 7th Marines cannot be overstated. The 1/7 was close to full strength, while the Marine units already on the island were badly depleted by casualties and disease.

The following day, a military correspondent confronted General Vandegrift. He claimed that the American people did not know what was happening on Guadalcanal, stating that they had been led to believe that the Marines were firmly in control and in possession of the island. The correspondent went on to say that with Vandegrift's troops confined to a small perimeter, that was far from true, and that he had heard that military leaders were about ready to give up on the Guadalcanal campaign. "Are you going to hold this beachhead?" the correspondent asked Vandegrift directly. "Are you going to stay here?" The general answered both questions with two words: "Hell, yes!"[31]

However, Marine commanders were aware that Japanese were making nightly runs to Guadalcanal, unloading both men and supplies. Their major concern was that of Japanese artillery being able to reach Henderson Field.

On September 21, Merritt Edson, having been promoted to colonel, assumed command of the 5th Marines and immediately began planning a move to rout the Japanese west of the Matanikau. What General Vandegrift and Colonel Edson did not know, but would soon learn, was that the Japanese had gathered about four thousand men to defend that position.[32]

CHAPTER 7

"DID THEY GET OFF?"

General Vandegrift experienced a boost in confidence after he received fresh troops and resupply. He now had more than nineteen thousand troops under his command with which to strengthen his defenses and expand his perimeter. To those ends, he unveiled Operational Plan 11-42, which divided his defenses into new sectors. The plan relieved the engineers with infantry battalions and filled the gaps that had existed south of Henderson Field. Marines and the Coast Guardsmen armed with bulldozers, barbed wire, sandbags, shovels, and captured machetes built a formative defensive ring. They carved out fields of fire up to one hundred yards and burned kunai grass to clear out even longer lanes between the U.S. artillery batteries and the enemy's cover. They chopped down trees in the coconut groves and used the logs to cover deeper and better fortified shelters. Adopting a trick learned from the Japanese, the

Americans planted grass on top of the logs for additional conceal-
ment. The grass grew quickly in the hot and humid environment,
and within a few days the logs were covered over. The Marines
taught the Coast Guardsmen how to string barbed wire, booby-
trap approaches with grenades, interlock guns, and place cans of
gasoline in trees that could be shot at, causing them to explode,
pressing cartridges into sandbags under their gun butts to mark the
exact spot to fire.[1]

The engineers resumed their normal duties during the day and
bolstered beach defenses at night. Each infantry regiment kept one
battalion in reserve. The fresh 7th Marines joined the 1st Marines,
who retained responsibility for the east side of the perimeter.

The plan also called for the perimeter to be extended beyond
the Matanikau on the west and the Tenaru on the east, thereby taking advantage of natural defenses blocking strengthened Japanese
movement toward main battle positions. Developing stronger positions west across the Matanikau was the top priority, however, and
required aggressive action.[2]

Despite the improvements in the U.S. perimeter defenses, the
enemy continued to conduct regular ambush attacks. The American commanders learned that the Japanese were strengthening
their own positions along the Matanikau. But they were not aware
that nearly four thousand Japanese troops were on the Matanikau
line, with reserves behind them. With Henderson Field reasonably
safe from attack, Vandegrift planned a series of actions to clear the
Matanikau of Japanese.

At 0500 on September 20, NOB Cactus received a report of
two downed American fliers from a Navy dive-bomber just off Savo
Island. The crew, consisting of Ensign Christopher Fink and his
gunner, Milo Kimberlin, were reported to be in a rubber boat between Savo Island and Cape Esperance. Armed only with a machine
gun and their Springfield rifles, a four-man volunteer crew consisting of Lieutenant Arthur Gibson, Coxswain Samuel B. Roberts,
Ray Evans, and Douglas Munro embarked in an open landing boat

to find the downed crew. Accompanying them was Master Sergeant James W. Hurlbut, a Marine Corps war correspondent. They soon arrived at the reported location, where four small Navy amphibious planes joined in the search. At about 0615, the rescue crew spotted the rubber boat. The planes circled over it, then headed back to their airfield. The rescue crew found the rubber boat empty with two paddles across the thwarts and a large hole in the bottom, evidence that something had happened to force the two men into the water. A strong tidal current moved diagonally from the south shore of Savo Island to Cape Esperance. Thinking the downed men had been carried ashore and captured, the rescue crew continued their search in that direction.[3]

Though they were methodical in their efforts, they saw no signs of the men during the hour it took to reach Cape Esperance. There, they noticed four large Japanese landing boats anchored at the west end of the beach. Nearly fifty feet long, painted black above the water and red below the waterline, each of these craft could reportedly carry one hundred Japanese soldiers. About a mile farther to the west, another group of boats were anchored offshore. Munro encouraged Lieutenant Gibson to move in for a closer look. Evans took up his position at the machine gun as Munro and Hurlbut stood at the gunwale with their rifles. Gibson ordered Roberts to move in slowly to a position about three hundred yards from both the boats and the shore. They noticed no sign of the Japanese. The only sound was that of their boat's engine. According to Hurlbut's account, Doug whispered, "They sure have a nice camp here. We ought to take it away from them."[4]

Just then the Japanese opened up with machine-gun fire. As the men took cover, Evans was hit by a ricocheting bullet in the right leg. Roberts turned the boat at full throttle and headed back out to sea. As they looked back, they could see at least four patterns of machine-gun fire churning up the water. According to Hurlbut's account, Evans yelled, "I'm going to take a crack at them," as he fired. The correspondent went on to write, "Tracer rounds raked the beach from one end to the other. Munro and I took several shots of our own with the rifles."[5]

Once they were safely out of range, Munro lowered his rifle and inspected the damage to their boat: twenty to thirty jagged rips inside and outside the boat and a surface wound to Evans's leg. When they returned to Lunga Point, they were advised that the two downed men had been picked up by one of the flying boats shortly before they had spotted the rubber boat.[6]

IN THE FIRST action along the Matanikau, Lieutenant Colonel "Chesty" Puller's 1st Battalion, 7th Marines (1/7) were to enter the Mount Austen area on September 23. Their orders were to cross the river upstream and patrol between the river and the village of Kokumbona by the twenty-sixth, at which time the 1st Raider Battalion would advance along the coast to the village and establish a permanent patrol base to prevent the Japanese from returning, thereby keeping Henderson Field out of range of Japanese artillery. With his Crusader's Cross around his neck, a jungle-stained copy of Julius Caesar's *The Gallic Wars* in his pocket, and his stump of a cold pipe clenched between his teeth, Chesty was right where he wanted to be, leading his Marines against the enemy. He would not have long to wait.

After they passed the perimeter on September 23, Puller's Marines surprised a Japanese force on the slopes of Mount Austen. The enemy was routed just after nightfall. The Marines gave much worse than they got, but still suffered seven killed and twenty-five wounded. Puller requested air support to continue his attack the following day and also asked for stretchers for his wounded.[7] When Vandegrift received Puller's request, he realized that evacuation of the wounded over the rugged terrain required at least a hundred able-bodied men. He sent the 2nd Battalion, 5th Marines (2/5) to reinforce Puller. Having received the reinforcements, Puller sent two companies to carry the wounded and provide security for the detail, then pushed on to the Matanikau. Vandegrift had given

Puller the option to alter the original patrol plan to if circumstances arose to prevent the unit from reaching its assigned patrol point by the target date, which was September 26. When the 1/7 and the 2/5 arrived at the river, they did not cross, but instead patrolled north along the east bank toward the coast.[8] As the Marines reached the mouth of the river, they drew fire from strong Japanese positions along the west bank. E and G Companies attempted to cross the river, but were pinned down by automatic-weapons fire. At the same time, unknown to the Marines, a Japanese company moved into a defensive position on the eastern end of the single-log bridge, known as Jap Bridge, which served as the only crossing upstream.[9] Over the next two hours, Puller's unit suffered twenty-five more casualties. He broke off the action and had his Marines strengthen their positions for the night. The Raider battalion, on its way to establish the patrol base at Kokumbona, had reached the area of the firefight and received orders to join with the 1/7 and the 2/5 to prepare for an attack the next day. Vandegrift sent Colonel Edson to take command and execute a revised plan that called for the Raiders to move two thousand yards inland, cross the Matanikau, and envelop the enemy right while the 1/7 provided covering fire and the 2/5 crossed the mouth of the river.[10]

Heavy rain fell throughout the night. The weight, volume, and ear-splitting noise of a tropical rain are likely beyond our experience. "The rain blurred vision and intensified the jungle gloom. Under its battering, men blinked and ducked . . . the ground beneath their feet became slippery and then viscous slime, and soon sucking, clotting mud."[11]

The attack started just after dawn on the twenty-seventh, but failed to gain momentum. The Marines of the 2/5 could not force a crossing of the Matanikau, and as the Raiders reached Jap Bridge they were met with heavy gunfire.[12] An attempt to swing around the Japanese blocking force and come down on its rear was detected by the Japanese, and the Raiders were pinned down.[13]

The radio message sent by the Raiders reporting the situation was either misinterpreted or incomplete. Edson believed that the Raiders had succeeded in gaining the enemy's right flank beyond the river and that the fight was in progress across the river. Proceeding on erroneous information, the Raider battalion and the 2/5 were ordered to resume their attack at 1330, while the 1/7 made an amphibious maneuver west of Point Cruz to strike the Japanese line along the Matanikau from the rear.[14]

Marine commanders approached Lieutenant Commander Dwight H. Dexter early on the morning of September 27 to coordinate the 1/7's amphibious landing. The plan called for a flotilla of Higgins boats and tank lighters to embark the Marines of the 1/7 under the command of Major Otho Rogers at Kukum and transport them to the head of a small cove on the eastern side of Point Cruz under covering fire from the destroyer *Ballard*. From there, the Marines were to drive straight inland. "Unfortunately, it did not turn out that way."[15]

After the operational briefing, Dexter placed Doug in charge of the operation. Doug, Ray, and the other coxswains spent the rest of the morning ensuring that all boats were fully operational and mission ready. Once Munro's boats were in position at about 1230, the Marines embarked. Doug and Ray were in separate boats, each equipped with an air-cooled Lewis .30-caliber machine gun and ammunition, with Doug's boat in the lead. Ray followed closely with Navy coxswain Samuel B. Roberts. About a mile offshore from their intended landing site, the boats rendezvoused with the *Ballard*, which began covering fire with its 5-inch guns. As the *Ballard* commenced firing, Doug began to lead the boats toward shore. Within minutes, a strong Japanese bombing raid came in from Rabaul. The Marine division command post was hit, and the communication equipment was heavily damaged. The *Ballard* ceased fire and took evasive action, its weapons directed toward the Japanese planes. Approximately a thousand yards offshore, Doug saw what appeared to be a coral reef that blocked their landing. Ray maneuvered his boat alongside Doug's, and both men quickly scanned the coast for a suitable alternate landing site. Both agreed that their only option was about a hundred yards up the coast on a very narrow beach. Ray informed Major Rogers that they would have to land on the right-hand side of the cove, and, after getting ashore, they would have to make a flanking maneuver to the left to maintain their plan. "As the boats landed, the beach was about eight feet wide, quite steep with immediate jungle growth. In some places the bows of the boats were actually in the jungle."[16]

What the Marines did not know was that the Japanese, anticipating an attack for three days, had prepared positions on the ridge overlooking the landing site. Waiting on the Marines were a battalion of Japanese infantry, coupled with a machine-gun platoon, a battalion infantry gun unit, and one-third of a battalion machine-gun unit.[17] Doug led his boats back to Lunga Point while Evans and Roberts remained just offshore to evacuate any immediate wounded. A quick burst of Japanese machine-gun fire struck the boat, severely damaging the throttle cable and gravely wounding Roberts. Evans slammed the throttle full and made his way back to Lunga Point. As he approached, Evans, unable to throttle back, hit the beach at about twenty knots, finally stopping about thirty feet onto the inclined shoreline. Munro ran toward the crippled boat as Evans yelled that Roberts had been hit. Munro jumped into the boat while corpsmen came running with medical supplies. Evans knew that young Roberts's injuries were life-threatening. Both men stood back while medics frantically tended to the unconscious coxswain. Munro and Evans just looked at each other. When the litter arrived, Munro and Evans helped the corpsmen get Roberts off the boat and to the base hospital.[18]

Back at the landing site, the Japanese waited until the Marines had reached the high ground about five hundred yards from the beach. "Suddenly, all hell broke loose; mortar and artillery fire seemed to be coming from everywhere."[19] Major Rogers was hit by a mortar round that killed him instantly and severely wounded

Captain Zach Cox. Command of the unit now fell to Captain Charles Kelly. A Japanese battalion counterattacked from Matanikau village. As the last Marines of the 1/7 cleared the beach, they saw the Japanese approaching. The Marines who were the last to clear the beach set up a machine gun and fired until they were overrun, at which time "the Marines were effectively cut off from the sea."[20] Kelly realized that his unit had no radio and therefore "no means to request supporting arms or even inform division of his plight."[21] The 2/5's F Company had failed to reach the far side of the river, and Kelly's unit, "surrounded and under attack by superior forces, was on the verge of reenacting Custer's Last Stand."[22] Desperate, Kelly's men spelled out the word "HELP" on the ground with their white undershirts.

Flying overhead in his dive-bomber was Lieutenant Dale Leslie, a Marine pilot who had been strafing and bombing Japanese positions at low levels, which drew the attention of the Japanese forces. Leslie saw the message and radioed it to division, which in turn relayed it to Edson's command post. Puller argued for an attack by the units on the east side of the river in an attempt to break through to his own outfit. Edson not only refused; he also authorized the Raiders to retreat. Puller was livid, and stated, "Most of my battalion will be out there alone, cut off without support. You're not going to throw these men away."[23]

Puller left the command post and walked to the beach, where he had a signalman contact the *Monssen*, which was just offshore. Puller took a launch out to the ship, where he explained the situation to the commanding officer, who agreed to assist. Familiar with the mechanics of naval firepower from previous billets, Puller met "with the gunnery officer, while the destroyer's captain contacted Lunga Point for landing craft."[24]

WITH ROBERTS EVACUATED, Munro and Evans walked slowly up the long pier toward the operations building, neither man saying a word. Just before they reached the end of the pier, they noticed

Commander Dexter running toward them waving a piece of paper. He was obviously yelling, but neither Evans nor Munro could hear what he was saying over the deep throttling of the engines as the boats refueled.

Munro looked at Evans and said, "Whatever he's yelling about, it ain't good." Evans replied, "Never is." Doug smiled.[25]

As Dexter reached the pair, he yelled, "Are you ready to go back and get those jarheads off that beach? They are getting hit pretty hard." Munro looked at Evans and said, "Hell, yeah!" Both turned and ran back down the pier, yelling to the other boat crews to get ready to depart. They jumped into their boat and prepared to shove off.[26]

PULLER, STILL ON board the *Monssen* offshore from his embattled Marines, "sent messages by blinker and semaphore flags to his troops ashore. Looking through his field glasses, he saw Sgt. Robert Raysbrook standing on the fire-swept ridge wigwagging a reply." Puller ordered the gunnery officer to "lay down a barrage between the coast and the ridge and then shift it to the flanks" as his Marines withdrew. After the men on the beach were notified, the *Monssen*'s guns let loose with thirty-eight 5-inch rounds. Due to the confusion caused by the *Monssen*'s barrage and the incessant Japanese mortar fire, the Marine column retreating toward the beach split up. Japanese troops rushed forward to exploit this mistake, and were able to cut off most of A Company. Platoon Sergeant Anthony Malanowski Jr. picked up a BAR from a wounded Marine and covered the withdrawing Marines until he was killed.[27]

WITH MUNRO AND Evans in the lead, the landing craft approached the extraction point. Around them, enemy mortar fire caused violent percussive eruptions of water that towered above the flat-bottomed boats, drenched the crews, and decreased both maneuverability and visibility. Withering automatic-weapons fire from the beach splintered several of the plywood-hulled boats and whizzed past the heads of the crews. As the enemy fire increased, one of the boat crews pulled their craft alongside Munro's. They yelled that a rescue attempt was too dangerous and suggested they all return to Lunga Point Base. Munro responded by jabbing his finger toward the beach and yelled, "We're not leavin' them there. We're goin' in!"[28]

Still in the lead, Munro maneuvered his craft parallel with the shore while Evans provided covering fire from one of the boat's two machine guns. Waves of haggard Marines ran from the beach into the water, dragging both the dead and the wounded, while more Marines poured onto the beach from the dense jungle. Clinging to the protected side of the boat, one wet, exhausted, and blood-covered Marine looked at Evans and said, "You came back, thank God, you came back." Evans pointed to Munro, who was maneuvering the boat. He then directed the Marine to one of the boats behind them as waterspouts raised by Japanese automatic-weapons fire spiked across the water between the boats. Evans immediately looked back to check on the Marine, who gave him a thumbs-up and scrambled into a boat.[29]

Within minutes, nearly five hundred vulnerable Marines had run into the water. Meanwhile, Japanese troops armed with mortars and automatic weapons had set up on the beach. Munro noticed that the men in the water were all but defenseless against the onslaught of bullets and mortar fire and maneuvered his boat so that it was between them and the beach, giving the Marines cover.[30] One of those Marines was Gunnery Sergeant John Basilone. Once in position, Munro jumped into the other gun turret. He and Evans continued to provide covering fire while the last of the Marines loaded into the other boats.[31]

With all boats apparently away, Munro turned the bow of his craft to begin the four-mile return trip to Lunga Point Base. It was then he saw that one of his boats was caught on a coral reef. Many of the Marines were back in the water, trying unsuccessfully to rock the boat loose. Munro maneuvered his craft alongside and called for a towrope to pull the boat loose. After several attempts, Munro's efforts were successful and the boat was freed. The exhausted Marines climbed back into the boat. During the rescue efforts, the Japanese had trained their mortars and automatic weapons on the boats, but both appeared to be out of range.[32]

As Munro pulled his boat in behind the one they had just freed, Evans saw a trail of waterspouts coming across the water directly toward them. Seeing that Doug was facing forward, Ray yelled, "Doug, get down."

Doug didn't move or acknowledge Ray's warning. A single round hit him in the back of the neck at the base of his skull and he fell to the floor of the landing craft.[33]

With Doug down and unconscious, Ray took the throttle and raced the boat as fast as it would go back to Lunga Point Base. After beaching the boat, Ray knelt down and cradled Doug's head in his lap. Opening his eyes, Doug looked up at Ray and asked, "Did they get off?" As Ray replied affirmatively, Douglas Albert Munro, two weeks shy of his twenty-third birthday, smiled and breathed his last, just after 1800.[34]

While corpsmen ran toward the boat, Ray, covered with his best friend's blood, sat with tears streaming down his face. After several minutes, Ray recalled, "I heard Dexter calling my name. I looked up and saw him standing over me. As he reached out, he said, 'Come on, son.' I laid Doug's head down and got up. He helped me out of the boat as the medics climbed in."[35] After the corpsmen removed Doug from the boat on a litter, Ray and Commander Dexter trailed behind. The corpsmen turned toward the hospital, and Ray started to follow them. "Dexter took me by the arm and said, 'There's nothing you can do. Go get cleaned up. I'll be by later.'"[36]

On September 27, 1942, in what was called the Second Matanikau, the Marine Raiders reported two killed and eleven wounded. The 2/5 suffered sixteen killed and sixty-eight wounded over the two days. Puller's unit lost twenty-four with thirty-two wounded. "The engagement was a clear defeat for the Marines, however, since they failed to achieve their objective and been forced to retire from the field. All concerned felt lucky to have escaped without greater bloodshed." Combined with the engagement on September 24, the 1/7 suffered ninety-one casualties, more than 10 percent of the battalion's complement, including the unit's executive officer and all rifle company commanders. It would be the Marines' only defeat on Guadalcanal.[37]

Word of Douglas Munro's actions spread rapidly throughout the embattled and beleaguered Marine ranks. At first, the report was that Munro was wounded, and there was general concern among those who had been pulled from the beaches as they reflected on how Munro's actions saved their lives. That concern quickly turned to genuine sorrow as word was received of his death. While the official record is not clear, Ray was told by Lieutenant Commander Dexter that he had received a radio message from Puller upon hearing the news of Munro's death. Marine correspondent James Hurlbut took the news of Doug's death very hard.[38]

The following day, Douglas Albert Munro was buried in Lunga Cemetery, Row 22, Grave 3.* After a prayer by the chaplain, palm branches were placed over the grave, which had been filled in with the volcanic dirt Doug had helped to secure. Ray placed a simple hand-carved wooden cross at the head of Doug's grave while Lieutenant Commander Dexter and a large number of Marines stood by silently. After the Marines had departed, Dexter gave Ray a few quiet minutes before putting his hand on Ray's shoulder. As Ray and his commanding officer walked slowly back to headquarters, Dexter said to him, "I'm afraid it doesn't get any better, son. I just got word that Roberts didn't make it. He died on the flight to New Hebrides." Ray said nothing.[39]

Decades later, Ray reflected on Doug's death. "I never had a friend like that since; not one that close," he said. "We were best

---

*Lunga Cemetery is also known as the Marine Cemetery in Lunga, the Guadalcanal Cemetery, and Flanders Field of the Pacific.

friends. He died doing what he loved to do, and that was helping people. That day he helped hundreds."[40]

The division's official report highlighted the "good judgment of senior commanders" in preventing a major catastrophe, but off the record there was considerable finger-pointing. One thing all agreed upon was that "individual heroism had saved the day."[41] Puller recommended several Marines for medals, including Lieutenant Leslie, Sergeant Raysbrook, Sergeant Malanowski, and two Navy coxswains. He officially praised the Coast Guard boat crews and the men on the *Monssen*.[42] Commander Dexter made medal recommendations of his own.

There were more hard-fought battles both on land and in the waters off the cost of Guadalcanal. In early November, Ray Evans and Dwight Dexter, completely debilitated by malaria, were transferred to the military hospital in Nouméa, New Caledonia, which served as the U.S. military headquarters in the South Pacific. After a few weeks of care and convalescence, Dexter was sent back to San Francisco for assignment, while Ray transferred to the USS *Argonne*, an attack transport anchored in the middle of Nouméa's harbor. The *Argonne* served as the flagship first of Admiral Ghormley and then Admiral Halsey during the battle of Guadalcanal. The day after he arrived on board, Ray was escorted to Halsey's wardroom, where the two men met for the first time. After a brief conversation with the admiral, Ray was taken to the ship's personnel office. There he was informed that Admiral Halsey had awarded him a field promotion to chief signalman.[43]

Major General Vandegrift and his Marines had been relieved in October 1942 by U.S. Army units under the command of Major General Alexander Patch. Unknown to American military strategists, by early December the Japanese navy realized further efforts and resources directed toward Guadalcanal were futile.[44] The size of the U.S. military-industrial complex and the resulting volume of men and matériel had begun to overwhelm Japan, which caused the Japanese High Command to shift priorities and divert ever-shrinking resources from Guadalcanal to New Guinea. In what was called Operation Ke, the Japanese landed a battalion of troops on Guadalcanal on January 14, 1943, to act as a rear guard during the complete evacuation of their 10,600-man garrison on the island. Guadalcanal was secured on February 9, 1943.

Both Tulagi and Guadalcanal were developed into major bases supporting the advance through the Solomon Islands. In addition to Henderson Field, two additional runways were developed at Lunga Point and Koli Point. Guadalcanal ended any further attempts at expansion by the Japanese and was the first step toward the eventual unconditional surrender of Japan.

CHAPTER 8

FIRST FAMILY OF THE COAST GUARD

During the early afternoon of Sunday, September 27, Edith was troubled. She and James had returned from church services and finished lunch when she suddenly became very restless. She knew that something was wrong, terribly wrong, with Douglas. As the minutes passed, her concern grew to anguish. James saw the expression on her face and her restlessness and asked her if something was wrong. She shared her thoughts and concerns, but after listening for several minutes, James did his best to reassure her that Douglas was fine. Edith was not convinced. Her anguish turned to dread, her thoughts all-consuming, and she could find no peace. She had no idea of her son's location or what he was doing, but she was sure of one thing: Something was very wrong. She grabbed her purse and told James she was going to church. James offered to drive, but she insisted on walking—alone. James initially resisted the idea, but he soon relented because their conversation only seemed to fuel her anxiety. She walked so briskly that several times she found herself running.[1]

As she entered the Holy Nativity Episcopal Church in South Cle Elum, her anxiety level was such that she could feel her heart beating inside her chest and her breathing was both rapid and labored. She walked to the front pew, sat down, and took a minute to compose herself before kneeling in prayer. After nearly an hour, her prayers turned into a one-way conversation with God, then returned to prayer, a cycle that continued over three hours.[2]

Just after 1800 hours, the anxiety she had felt so strongly had subsided and she felt inner peace. She felt that whatever had been wrong was now right. She got up and slowly walked down the aisle and out the door into the cool evening air, then headed home.[3]

A HALF A world away, Lieutenant Commander Dwight Dexter had an important letter to write. A letter that would alter the recipients' lives forever. A letter no one wants to write and no one wants to receive. Alone with a cup of coffee at his desk, he began writing:

Believe me when I say sincerely that this is a very sad letter for me to write advising you of the death of your son Douglas, but as Commanding Officer of the unit to which he was attached at the time of his death, I have pride in telling you that he covered himself with honor and I hope Glory, and fulfilled the mission so satisfactorily that almost all of the men he had under his charge returned to their unit and without exception all had praise for your son's execution of his duties. It was a year ago last June that Douglas and Raymond Evans came to me and asked if they could be transferred to Captain Ashe's staff on board the Hunter Liggett. I succeeded in getting them and since that day have felt like Douglas was one of my boys, for with the exception of

one month when he was on the staff on board the McCawley,
both Douglas and Ray Evans have been with me and his loss
has left a very decided space which I feel will never be filled
so far as I am concerned.[4]

Lieutenant Commander Dexter continued to describe Doug's actions. After informing the Munros that his letter could not serve as official notification, he asked them to "keep it confidential until such time as the official notification is received . . . I consider this a personal letter and not an official report." Upon completing the letter, he gave it to his yeoman to type for his signature.

Later that afternoon, he found the letter on his desk under his pen. He signed it and handed it to the yeoman. What Dexter did not know at the time was that apparently the yeoman had typed a copy of the letter and forwarded it to Lieutenant Colonel Puller and the Marine Corps.[5]

In Cle Elum, many townspeople, along with the Munro family and their friends, were delighted to read an article by Master Sergeant James W. Hurlbut, the Marine war correspondent, that appeared in the *Seattle Times* on October 15, 1942. In the article, Hurlbut described the heroic actions of Ray and Doug on September 20. Edith later always described this as the "first episode."

The excitement of the Munro family was shattered late in the afternoon of October 19. As Edith looked out her living room window, she saw three uniformed officers, two Navy and one Coast Guard, approaching her front door. She backed away from the window and steadied herself against a piece of furniture. She heard the knock on the door but refused to answer. A second knock also went unanswered. However, James heard the knocking in the rear of the house. As he walked into the living room, Edith told him about the three men outside, and begged him not to answer the door. After the third knock, both Edith and James, holding on to each other, opened the door.[6]

The Coast Guard officer introduced himself and requested permission to come inside. Both Edith and James stepped aside to let them in. As the officers entered, they removed their hats. The Coast Guard officer introduced the accompanying officers and informed them of Doug's death, his burial on Guadalcanal, and that he had saved the lives of five hundred Marines, adding that they would receive official written notification from the Coast Guard and the War Department. The men extended their sympathies and departed.[7]

Edith was able to refrain from breaking down until the officers drove away; then the agonized tears flowed. James was stunned and sank into a chair. Edith was inconsolable. After several minutes, James called Doug's sister, Patricia, who lived in Seattle, to tell her the news. There was little sleep for the Munro family that night.[8]

The following day, Patricia arrived early in the morning to be with her mother. As the railroad substation's chief operator, James had to go to work; once there, he discovered that working occupied his mind and kept his thoughts off of the tragedy they had all suffered.[9]

Later that day, Lieutenant Commander Dexter's letter arrived in the mail. Edith began to read it, but only got as far as "advising you of the death of your son Douglas." Unable to continue, she handed it to Patricia, who read it aloud slowly. With tears streaming down the faces of both women, Edith read and reread the letter several times, pressing it to her lips, which stained the paper with lipstick and left small round spots indicative of the tears shed by a mother for her lost child. Apparently anticipating the parental "how" and "why" questions of their son's death, Lieutenant Commander Dexter explained the circumstances surrounding Doug's final action.

On Sunday the 27th of September an expedition was sent into an area where trouble was to be expected. Douglas was in charge of the ten boats which took the men down. In the latter part of the afternoon the situation had not developed as had been anticipated and in order to save the expedition it became necessary to send the boats back to evacuate the expedition. Volunteers were called for and true to the highest traditions of the Coast Guard and also to the traditions with which you had imbued your son was among the first to volunteer and was put in charge of the detail. The evacuation was as successful as could be hoped for under fire. But as always happens, the last men to leave the beach are the hardest pressed because they have been acting as the covering agent for the withdrawal of the other men, and your son knowing this so placed himself and his boats so that he could act as the covering agent for the last men, and by his action and successful maneuvers brought back a far greater number of men than had been even hoped for. He received his wound just as the last men were getting in the boats and clearing the beach. Upon regaining consciousness his only question was "Did they get off?", and so died with a smile on his face and the full knowledge that he had successfully accomplished a dangerous mission.[10]

While grief-stricken over the loss of her only son, she recalled the last words Doug spoke to her before returning to duty from leave: "Don't worry about me, Mother. I'm afraid of nothing and nobody." The fact that he died with a smile on his face provided a small amount of comfort for both Edith and Patricia. When James arrived home later that day, Edith quietly handed him the lipstick- and tear-stained letter. James slowly settled into a chair to read it. When he was finished, James let the letter fall into his lap, dropped his head back against the chair, and stared at ceiling. The only sound was that of the women sobbing. Heartbroken at the loss of his son, James clung to Dexter's words: "He was the true type of American Manhood that is going to win this war."[11]

As word spread across the small town of Doug's death, flowers, cards, and food began to arrive at the Munro home, often just left at the front door. Such compassionate gestures from the community were continuous over the next several days.[12]

The next day, the official telegram from the Coast Guard commandant, Admiral Russell R. Waesche, arrived. Reverend H. Lester Mather called on the family, and with their permission he and other members of the church organized a memorial service to be held on November 1. An article that provided the known details of Doug's final actions appeared in the *Seattle Times* on October 22. Two members of the local American Legion chapter stood silently on either side of the Munro's front door as a steady stream of family, friends, veterans, and sympathizers continued through the day on Saturday. Several visitors placed small American flags in the front yard.[13]

On November 1, James, Edith, and Patricia arrived at the Episcopal church. American flags lined the front walkway, and nearly every seat in the sanctuary was full for the regular Sunday morning service. Two members of the American Legion met the family at the doors and escorted Edith and Patricia to the only vacant seats, in the front pew, while James followed closely behind. Reverend Mather acknowledged Doug and the entire Munro family in his sermon, which had the idea of sacrifice as its theme. The memorial service was scheduled for one hour after the morning service. During the time between services, James, Edith, and Patricia accepted the condolences of hundreds of people, many of whom the family did not recognize.[14]

Reverend Mather began the memorial service by welcoming the large crowd and acknowledging those who were standing. Patricia instinctively turned toward the back of the church and saw a standing-room-only crowd that extended around both sides of the pews and about one-third of the way up the center aisle. Patricia whispered a comment to her parents and Edith began to sob. James turned and acknowledged the crowd. What the Munro family did not know then was that the church doors remained open to accommodate the crowd, which extended down the front steps and filled the front yard. Edith later stated that she recalled very little of what was said during the service.[15] In her program, she had kept a poem by Laurence Binyon entitled "For the Fallen":

> *They shall not grow old,*
> *As we that are left grow old.*
> *Age shall not weary them,*
> *Nor the years condemn.*
> *At the going down of the sun,*
> *and in the morning,*
> *We will remember them.*[16]

At the conclusion of the service, the crowd stood quietly as the Munro family was escorted down the center aisle; the only sound was that of the sobs of the mourners. Those standing in the center aisle parted to allow the family to pass. It was only when the family reached the back of the church that they realized the size of the crowd. As they exited and stood on the top step, they saw Boy Scouts, members of the American Legion and the Veterans of Foreign Wars, some in uniform, as well as members of the Sons of the American Legion, all carrying American flags. Members of the Washington State Guard lined both sides of the front sidewalk and snapped to attention as the family descended the steps. Patricia and Edith walked arm in arm while James walked several steps behind, thanking members of the crowd as he passed.[17]

What the Munro family and those gathered at the memorial service did not know that day was that a Medal of Honor recommendation file for Douglas Albert Munro was making its way up the chain of command. Lieutenant Commander Dexter conjectured that his yeoman must have given a copy of his letter to the Munros to someone at Marine Corps headquarters and that Marine legend Chesty Puller penned the Medal of Honor recommendation, which was signed by Major General Alexander A. Vandegrift. According to Dexter, a copy of his letter was in the recommendation file.

Edith later learned that about the same time she was over-come with fear and spent hours at the church, Doug was involved in what she later described as the "second episode" and was killed in action at 1800 hours. With her son no longer in pain or danger, Edith felt her inner peace.[18]

BACK ON GUADALCANAL, the battle continued. During the last week of September and the first week of October, the Japanese reinforced their position on the island with fresh troops, resupplies of food and ammunition, and increased air attacks on Henderson Field. Lieutenant General Millard Harmon, commander of the United States Army forces in the South Pacific, had convinced Admiral Ghormley, in one of his last command decisions, to reinforce the marines on Guadalcanal to properly defend the island and prepare for the next Japanese offensive.

During the period of October 1–18, the Japanese delivered nearly fifteen thousand troops to Guadalcanal. However, on October 6–9, in another action along the Matanikau River, Lieutenant Colonel Puller's 7th Marines inflicted heavy losses on the enemy, which hindered Japanese plans for an offensive against the U.S. forces at Lunga Point. On October 8, more than twenty-eight hundred men of the 164th Infantry Regiment sailed for Guadalcanal, escorted by the cruisers and destroyers of Task Force 64. On October 11–12, the task force successfully engaged Japanese cruisers and destroyers in what would be later known as the Battle of Cape Esperance.

BACK IN WASHINGTON, D.C., Admiral Nimitz and War Department leaders had lost all confidence in Admiral Ghormley's ability to command and ordered Admiral William F. "Bull" Halsey to report to the USS *Argonne*, anchored in the harbor at Nouméa, New Heb-rides, on October 17. After Halsey's plane landed near the *Argonne*, a motor whaleboat drew alongside. As Halsey stepped on board, a young lieutenant, junior grade stepped up, saluted, and handed the admiral a sealed envelope marked SECRET. Halsey opened the envelope, read the two-line message, then handed it to his Marine adviser, Colonel Julian Brown. It said, YOU WILL TAKE COMMAND OF THE SOUTH PACIFIC AREA AND SOUTH PACIFIC FORCES IMMEDIATELY.

Halsey and Ghormley were good friends, so the order to relieve him was disconcerting to Halsey. To both men's chagrin, no one informed Ghormley of the command change; he learned of it only when Admiral Halsey arrived.

On Guadalcanal, Japanese forces conducted numerous unsuccessful assaults against Puller's Marines and the Army's 164th Infantry Regiment late on October 24. Subsequent Japanese attacks near the Matanikau were also repelled with the heavy Japanese losses. To exploit their victories, on November 1, Major General Vandegrift dispatched six Marine battalions and one Army battalion to initiate an offensive west of the Matanikau.

After Doug's death, Ray had been assigned as a coxswain to the coastwatcher Martin Clemens and his men, who were conducting nighttime reconnaissance missions. But both Ray and Lieutenant Commander Dexter suffered incapacitating relapses of malaria and were scheduled to be medically evacuated. Just before their evacuation on November 9, the two men walked the short distance to Lunga Cemetery, Row 22, Grave 3. They noticed that all handmade markers had been replaced with concrete crosses and bases bearing each man's name, service branch, and date of death. According to Ray, he and Dexter traded a few "Doug stories." He recalled that the lieutenant commander told the story of Doug's appearance when he reported for duty at Cactus, saying, "He was a sight, I'll say that, but I was glad to get him . . . glad to have you both." After several minutes of stories, they bowed their head in silent prayer. Then they walked back to Dexter's headquarters.[19]

Late that afternoon, Ray and Lieutenant Commander Dexter transferred to the *Hunter Liggett*, which was anchored offshore. Safely on board, Dexter was immediately taken to sick bay by Navy corpsmen. Ray turned and took one last, prolonged look at the island where the two best friends had arrived three months ago; today, only one was leaving. He could see Red Beach, where he and his fellow coasties had landed so many Marines. To the left was a green lagoon and sandpit known as the Tenaru. To his right was Henderson Field. As he looked farther to the right, west of Lunga Lagoon was the mouth of the Matanikau, and farther west was Point Cruz, where he had lost his shipmate Samuel Roberts and his best friend Doug. Like the Rising Sun of Japan, he saw the red sun sink behind Cape Esperance and into the Pacific. The next day, he boarded a float plane and transferred to the *Argonne*.[20]

Following three days of complete bed rest, proper nutrition, and antimalarial medication, Ray was unexpectedly escorted to the bridge to meet with Admiral Halsey. Ray remembered that "he said he appreciated Doug and my efforts, was disappointed to hear of Doug's death, that our actions saved hundreds of good men, and said that we were both fine examples for others to follow." He was directed to go to the yeoman's office, and then the meeting was over. Ray recalled that "the only chief petty officer's coat I could find to wear was that of a carpenter's mate, so I wore the left-armed chief carpenter's rate until I could get to Treasure Island in San Francisco and buy a uniform."[21]

Lieutenant Commander Dexter was transferred to San Francisco and spent six weeks in the hospital. Ray and Dexter would later reunite.

In Cle Elum, Edith tried to channel her energies into something constructive with a connection to Doug's life of service. She had learned from Coast Guard officials that President Roosevelt would sign Public Law 773 on November 23. It would amend the Coast Guard Auxiliary and Reserve Act of 1941 "to expedite the war effort by providing for releasing officers and men for duty at sea and their replacement by women in the shore establishment of the Coast Guard, and for other purposes." Selected to lead the new unit was Dorothy C. Stratton, a lieutenant in the Women's Reserve who was on leave from Purdue University, where she was a professor and a dean of women. For the name of the new unit, which was modeled after the Women's Army Auxiliary Corps (WAAC) and the Navy's Women Accepted for Volunteer Emergency Service (WAVES),

Stratton created the acronym SPAR, from the Coast Guard's Latin motto *Semper Paratus*, which has the English translation "Always Ready." After talking with Coast Guard officials, Edith thought that the SPARs would keep her connected to her son and provide a way for her to continue his legacy of service to both the country and the Coast Guard. While she intended to enlist, Coast Guard officials offered her a direct reserve commission with the advanced rank of lieutenant, junior grade. She accepted the commission on the condition that she would be permitted to attend and complete the six-week officer training at the Coast Guard Academy, like any other officer candidate, prior to formally accepting her commission. Coast Guard officials agreed.[22]

IN LATE NOVEMBER, the Japanese forces on Guadalcanal faced critical food shortages, and Japanese commanders were losing about fifty men per day from disease, malnutrition, and U.S. air and ground attacks. On Thanksgiving Day, 1942, while the haggard Marines ate their turkey and cranberry sauce, were notified that in early December they would be relieved by Army troops and sent to Australia for rest and reorganization. Command of the forces on Guadalcanal passed from Major General Alexander Vandegrift to General Alexander Patch on December 9.

On December 12, Japan's top naval commanders proposed that Guadalcanal be abandoned, and in late December ordered their staffs to draft plans for the rapid withdrawal of all Japanese forces in what was called Operation Ke, scheduled to begin the latter part of January.

In late December, the 1st Marine Division, which had been on the front lines for more than four months, began going out to its transports. As they made their way down to the beach to board the boats, many were heavily bearded, ragged, with barely the strength to walk, but each had made his way to the cemetery where many of their comrades were at rest to pay their last respects. Once alongside the transports, many could not ascend the cargo nets and were hoisted on board on stretchers.

On February 4, 1943, the last Japanese troops were removed from Guadalcanal under the cover of darkness. The American victory on Guadalcanal was now complete. Guadalcanal was the first prolonged campaign and the first U.S. offensive of the war in the Pacific. It ended all attempts at Japanese expansion and placed the Allies in a position of supremacy. Guadalcanal became a major air and naval base. As one of the last Marines to leave Guadalcanal on March 15, 1943, Master Sergeant James W. Hurlbut visited Doug Munro's gravesite in what the Marines called Flanders Field and penned a letter to his father, James. He wrote: "Doug was one of the finest men I have met in the service—kind, courteous, thoughtful, and, above all, courageous. His death, even in a place where death was commonplace, shocked me. . . . Doug gave his life in an effort to save the lives of others. . . . Even though Doug was killed, the boats got in and many men who would otherwise have been lost were saved. Believe me, Doug is one of the <u>real</u> heroes of this war."[23]

As THE ANNUAL thaw began to melt the snow and swell the rivers of the nearby Cascades in the spring of 1943, Edith sat in her kitchen alone with her thoughts, the silence broken only by the familiar morning songs of the birds outside her kitchen window. Her thoughts were of her lost son. As she slowly walked back into what was Doug's room, the ring of the telephone startled her. She used the several steps to the telephone in the kitchen to catch her breath before answering.

"Hello," Edith said softly.

"Mrs. Munro?" a deep male voice inquired.

"Yes." Her pulse and breath quickened.

"Ma'am, this is Coast Guard Headquarters. I am honored to inform you that your son has been recommended for the Medal of Honor. We are waiting on a final decision by President Roosevelt." The speaker then cautioned her against making any comment about the matter, public or private, and was told that she would be notified when additional information was available.[24]

"Thank you" was the only reply she could muster as her eyes filled with tears, which flowed freely down her face. Hanging up the phone, she reached for and settled into the nearest chair. Trembling and sobbing, she buried her face in her hands for several minutes before taking a napkin from the table to dry her face and eyes. Then she gathered her coat and walked out the front door. The brisk breeze against her moist eyes startled her as she walked the short distance to James's office next door.[25]

James was surprised to see his wife standing in the doorway. He quickly stood and, seeing that she had been crying, asked her what was wrong as he guided her to a chair. She told him of the telephone call from the Coast Guard. James was extremely proud of Doug's service and appreciated the significance of the Medal of Honor and his son's place in military history. That evening, James telephoned Patricia to inform her of the news and cautioned her against saying anything until they were notified by the Coast Guard.[26]

Later that week, in response to a local newspaper editorial by Royal Brougham, James sent two of Doug's harmonicas to the newspaper office and suggested they be donated to servicemen. Within days of the arrival of the harmonicas, the following editorial, again written by Brougham, appeared.

Mr. Munro, a reporter was griping at the new rationing regulations when your note and package arrived. He said that this lousy war would ruin everybody's stomach. The makeup market was giving the government a good cussing . . . do the dopes back in Washington want to drive everyone over the hill to the poorhouse? The baseball writer's gas tank went dry on the way to the office, and he was so burned that smoke was coming out his ears. We all agreed that the war was messing up everything something awful. Then the little brunette who distributes the mail since the office boys have all gone into the service brought your little package. We opened it, read the note about your boy, Doug. Mr. Munro, you never saw a more shamed and sheepish crowd of news-men in your life. Who were we to be talking about sacrifices? Sir, we're going to ask a favor. We're going to buy a whole flock of new mouth organs for the boys in the service, but we want to keep your little offering in the top drawer of the desk . . . and the next squawker who comes in to bellyache about rationing and taxes, we're going to take out the little box. We're going to show him the token from a father who sacrificed his son "Doug" for his country, and then gave up the boy's harmonicas so as to make army life a little more pleasant for some music-hungry soldier.[27]

James's gesture and the subsequent editorial started a firestorm of support as donations of musical instruments, including pianos, were offered. The newspaper arranged for the Northwest Camp and Hospital Service Council's armory to receive and distribute the donations. In the April 1943 edition of *Coast Guard Magazine*, Edith wrote: "At first the news of his death seemed unbearable, but as time goes on we begin to see that his life's mission was finished on this [E]arth, and that he more than earned his way to whatever paradise awaits. I would like you to know that it was the very high traditions of the Coast Guard Service, the saving and preserving of life, which definitely decided Douglas to enter the Coast Guard Service . . . and [this] has been and will continue to be a great comfort to his father and myself."[28]

In Washington, D.C., Puller's Medal of Honor recommendation for Signalman First Class Douglas Albert Munro rested on President Roosevelt's desk. Per the Navy chain of command and Medal of Honor recommendation process in effect during World War II, it had received the support and signatures of Admiral William F. Halsey, Commander of the South Pacific Area; Admiral Chester W. Nimitz, Commander in Chief, Pacific Fleet; Admiral Ernest J. King, Commander in Chief, U.S. Fleet and Chief of Naval Operations; Admiral Russell R. Waesche, Commandant of the

Coast Guard; Admiral William D. Leahy, Chairman of the Joint Chiefs of Staff; and Frank Knox, Secretary of the Navy.

On or about May 1, the Coast Guard and the Navy notified James and Edith that Douglas's recommendation for the Medal of Honor had been approved by President Roosevelt and that a White House Oval Office ceremony was planned for noon on Tuesday, May 27, 1943. They would be contacted by the Coast Guard to make arrangements for a formal escort from Seattle to Washington, D.C. With the date and time of the White House ceremony set, the Coast Guard planned a formal ceremony for Edith Munro to accept her commission. It was scheduled for 1400 hours, following the White House ceremony. The Munro family traveled to Washington, D.C. by train in a private car accompanied by their Coast Guard escort.[29]

Just before noon on May 27, the family was escorted into the Oval Office for a private meeting with the president. There, seated behind his desk with the characteristic black cigarette holder clenched between his teeth, President Roosevelt warmly greeted them. After a short conversation, a military aide read the citation.

For extraordinary heroism and conspicuous gallantry above and beyond the call of duty as Petty Officer in Charge of a group of 24 Higgins boats, engaged in the evacuation of a battalion of marines trapped by enemy Japanese forces at Point Cruz Guadalcanal, on 27 September 1942. After making preliminary plans for the evacuation of nearly 500 beleaguered marines, Munro, under constant strafing by enemy machineguns on the island, and at great risk of his life, daringly led 5 of his small craft toward the shore. As he closed the beach, he signaled the others to land, and then in order to draw the enemy's fire and protect the heavily loaded boats, he valiantly placed his craft with its 2 small guns as a shield between the beachhead and the Japanese. When the perilous task of evacuation was nearly completed,

Munro was instantly killed by enemy fire, but his crew, 2 of whom were wounded, carried on until the last boat had loaded and cleared the beach. By his outstanding leadership, expert planning, and dauntless devotion to duty, he and his courageous comrades undoubtedly saved the lives of many who otherwise would have perished. He gallantly gave his life for his country.[30]

As White House and military photographers knelt in front of the desk, cameras at the ready, President Roosevelt awarded the Medal of Honor posthumously to Douglas A. Munro; his parents accepted the nation's highest military award on his behalf. After several minutes of conversation and photographs, the Munro family was escorted to Coast Guard headquarters, where Edith, having recently graduated from the Coast Guard Academy, changed into her dress uniform and stood before the commandant and other high-ranking Coast Guard officials. With flashbulbs popping, she raised her right hand and, at the age of forty-eight, repeated the same oath of office taken by her son four years earlier: "I, Edith F. Munro, do solemnly swear that I will support and defend the Constitution of the United States against all enemies, foreign and domestic; that I will bear true faith and allegiance to the same; that I take this obligation freely, without any mental reservation or purpose of evasion; and that I will well and faithfully discharge the duties of the office on which I am about to enter. So help me God. And I do further swear that I will use by best endeavors to prevent and detect frauds against the laws of the United States imposing duties upon imports. So help me God."[31]

After the ceremony, Edith was asked by members of the press corps why she had joined the SPARs. She replied, "We are a Coast Guard family, through Doug. He loved his service. I am very happy to be eligible to serve in it."[32]

Her first assignment was on the staff of the commandant as a public affairs officer in Washington, D.C. She traveled throughout the country telling the story of her son, talking about the Coast Guard, and recruiting women for the SPARs. After six months, desiring to make a more direct impact, she requested a transfer closer to home and was assigned to the 13th Coast Guard District in Seattle, where Doug had originally enlisted, and was placed in charge of the SPAR barracks at the Assembly Hotel in Seattle. She also was the first women to serve on a Coast Guard district command staff. In addition to her assigned duties, she continued to attend many ceremonial Coast Guard functions throughout the country.[33]

Edith's family had a long history of military and public service. In addition to her and James's military service, her father, William Joseph Thrower Fairey, served as a corporal in the 15th Lancashire Rifle Regiment in 1877. Her brother Leonard served in the 11th Canadian Mounted Rifles and subsequently as a Member of Parliament from Victoria, Canada. Her sister Mary lost a son when the HMCS *Guysborough*, a *Bangor*-class minesweeper, was sunk by a German U-boat while escorting an Allied merchant convoy off the coast of France on March 17, 1945; the other fifty crew members were lost as well. A nephew, William Lane Fairey Jr., had been a Japanese prisoner of war on Wake Island before being rescued by American troops. His father, Leonard Thrower Fairey Sr., was in charge of road paving on the island when it was seized by the Japanese in 1941. When it came time for the Americans on the island to evacuate, there was not enough room on the planes, so Bill volunteered to be captured so that his father could escape. Many other nieces and nephews served in the military or went on to public service careers as teachers and doctors.[34]

The impact of Doug's sacrifice was reinforced to the family on June 15, 1943, when Edith received a heartfelt letter from a Mrs. G. Van Wyck of New York, the mother of one of the Marines Doug rescued, stating, ". . . your son saved . . . my son . . . who had almost given up hope of being rescued . . ." Edith also received a touching letter from the diocesan bishop recognizing Doug's Medal of Honor on July 3.[35]

First Lady Eleanor Roosevelt visited the Lunga Cemetery on September 17, 1943. Prior to her visit, islanders had erected a thatched-roof chapel, beautified the grounds, and decorated the gravesites. Video footage of the visit showed a moved First Lady as she slowly and respectfully walked row by row past each of the concrete crosses with her head bowed. She later recorded memories of her visit in a diary entry.

Having been previously contacted by leaders of Doug's Boy Scout Troop 84, James donated Doug's handmade pack board, which served as the annual "traveling" trophy for the troop's outstanding camper. Doug's parents presented the first Douglas Munro Outstanding Camper Award on December 8.[36]

Edith Munro was promoted to lieutenant on July 1, 1944. Ten days later, she served as the sponsor at the commissioning ceremony of the Navy's newest ship. The USS *Douglas A. Munro* was a *John C. Butler*-class destroyer used primarily as an escort to protect ships in convoy as well as other assigned tasks, such as patrol or serving as a radar picket (to increase radar-detection range around a force to protect it from surprise enemy attack and to direct friendly fighters intercepting the enemy). The *Munro*'s first assignment was as an escort for the USS *Vixen*, a gunboat that served as the flagship of Admiral Royal E. Ingersoll, the commander in chief of the Atlantic Fleet, on a tour of Caribbean defenses. Following that deployment, the ship served as an escort for the escort carrier USS *Kasaan Bay* on a voyage to Casablanca.

IN THE SOUTH Pacific, Allied naval and ground forces had retaken the Gilbert and Marshall Islands, along with Saipan, from the Japanese and were making their way through the Mariana and Palau Islands. U.S. naval forces decisively defeated the IJN in the three-day (June 19–21, 1944) Battle of the Philippine Sea, also known as the Great Marianas Turkey Shoot due to the disproportionate losses suffered by the Japanese. The Japanese lost three carriers and more than six hundred aircraft in the battle, which eliminated the IJN's ability to conduct large-scale carrier-based operations.

The first American use of napalm occurred during the Battle of Tinian (July 24–August 1, 1944). Tinian was another decisive U.S. victory; Japanese losses exceeded eight thousand. The island became the camp for fifty thousand U.S. troops and the site of the most heavily used airfield of the war, playing a critical part in ending the war with Japan.

American victories at both Peleliu and Angaur set the stage for one of the war's most famous battles. During Operation Stalemate II, the code-name for the Peleliu campaign (September–November 1944), the 1st Marine Division and subsequently the Army's 81st Infantry Division successfully battled the Japanese for control of the island's airstrip. At Angaur, an island in the Palau chain, a battle was fought from September 19 to October 22, 1944. Part of the larger campaign known as Operation Forager, the battle was the rare occasion when American losses exceeded those of the Japanese. During the fighting, Navy Seabees constructed an airfield that housed B-24 Liberator bombers, enabling American planes to bomb the remaining Palau Islands as well as the Philippines.

WHILE DOUG'S COAST Guard and Navy colleagues maintained their efforts in the Pacific, Edith continued her duties ashore. Following her command of the SPAR barracks, she assumed the duties of personnel officer in the Women's Reserve in January 1945. Although Seattle was her permanent duty station, Lieutenant Munro performed temporary duty in Long Beach, California; Houston, Texas; Philadelphia, Pennsylvania; and Washington, D.C.[37]

OPERATION DETACHMENT, CODE name for the Battle of Iwo Jima, was fought between February 16 and March 26, 1945. It resulted in some of the fiercest and bloodiest fighting of the war. Although both sides sustained heavy losses, America's overwhelming number of arms and complete air superiority, coupled with the impossibility of Japanese retreat or reinforcement, assured a U.S. victory from the onset of the initial amphibious landings. The battle was immortalized by Joseph Rosenthal's iconic photograph of the raising of the American flag on top of Mount Suribachi.

In Europe, with the Fascist government of Italy having already surrendered, the Allies accepted the full and unconditional surrender of Nazi Germany's Third Reich on May 8, 1945, which was President Harry S. Truman's sixty-first birthday. Adolph Hitler committed suicide during the Battle of Berlin, so the surrender was authorized by his successor, German president Karl Dönitz, in Berlin. With the war in Europe now over, the U.S. military turned its full attention to the defeat of Japan, although the outcome of the war had been determined on Guadalcanal.

Having fulfilled her two-year enlistment, Lieutenant Edith Munro announced her retirement from active duty on May 25, 1945. During World War II, the Munro family sacrificed Douglas, its only male heir, to the war effort, while James served with the Washington State Guard Reserve and Edith served on active duty military. However, the family's service and commitment to the Coast Guard was far from over.[38]

CHAPTER 9

COMING HOME

The military strategy of island hopping by the United States was extremely effective. U.S. forces had not lost a battle in the Pacific since the victory on Guadalcanal, and by June 1, 1945, the military situation clearly favored the Allied cause. The Philippines had been retaken in February, Iwo Jima was under American control, Germany had surrendered in May, and troops in Europe would soon be available for redeployment to the Pacific. Victory on Okinawa was assured, Allied air and submarine attacks had all but severed Japan from its critically needed resources from the Indies, Allied precision bombing from the Marianas were leveling Japan's cities and industrial sites, and Allied submarines and the mining of Japanese coastal waters had nearly destroyed the Japanese merchant fleet. In fact, the Japanese had suffered an unbroken string of defeats for nearly two years in the South Pacific. As a result, the Japanese civilian economy had deteriorated to disastrous levels. Coupled with the worst rice harvest since 1909, malnutrition and starvation were widespread. Earlier in the year, Prince Fumimaro Konoe advised Emperor Hirohito that defeat was inevitable and urged him to surrender.[1]

In stark contrast to its condition after nearly Pearl Harbor four years prior, the U.S. Pacific Fleet had risen like a phoenix from the ashes and driven the Imperial Japanese Navy from the Pacific, while fast-carrier aircraft were striking Japanese naval bases in the Inland Sea.

In Washington, plans were under way for Operation Downfall, the invasion of the Japanese mainland with Okinawa as the staging area. Comprised of two parts, Operations Olympic and Coronet, the invasion was set to begin in October. First, during Operation Olympic, a series of landings would be staged by the U.S. Sixth Army in effort to capture the southern third of the southernmost main island of Kyūshū. Operation Olympic was to be followed by Operation Coronet in March 1946; its objective was the capture of the Kantō Plain, near Tokyo on the island of Honshū, by the U.S. First, Eighth, and Tenth Armies.[2]

Despite staggering losses and their fate resting off the shores of their mainland, the Japanese Supreme Council for the Direction of the War, known as the "Big Six"—composed of Prime Minister Kantarō Suzuki, Minister of Foreign Affairs Shigenori Tōgō, Minister of the Army Korechika Anami, Minister of the Navy Mitsumasa Yonai, Chief of the Army General Staff Yoshijirō Umezu, and Chief of the Navy General Staff Koshirō Oikaka—gave no consideration to unconditional surrender. Japanese troops had demonstrated throughout the war that they would inflict heavy casualties and literally fight to the last man.

Allied intelligence reported that Japan had ample reserves of arms and ammunition and a remaining army of 5 million, of which 2 million were on the home island and could be expected to initiate a strong defense. The Japanese army had made elaborate preparations for the defense of the Japanese mainland. In the opinion of intelligence experts, neither blockade nor bombing alone would initiate the unconditional surrender before March 1, 1946, the date set for the Allied invasion.[3]

American military leaders were alarmed by the Japanese buildup. Secretary of War Henry Stimson was concerned about the exceptionally high number of probable American casualties. A special report estimated that the invading Allies would suffer between 1.7 and 4 million casualties, of whom between 400,000 and 800,000 would be killed, while Japanese casualties would be around 5 to 10 million.[4]

Concurrent with the planning of Operation Downfall, the top secret Allied Manhattan Project, originally begun in 1939 near Los Alamos, New Mexico, was nearing completion. The first atomic bombs were initially targeted for use against Germany, but that country's surrender in May 1945 changed the focus to Japan. In preparation, Project Alberta was initiated and the 509th Composite Group was activated in December 1944, under the command of Colonel Paul Tibbets at the Wendover Army Air Field in Utah. The 509th was provided with fifteen Silverplate B-29s, specially adapted to carry specialized payloads and equipped with fuel-injected engines, Curtis Electric reversible-pitch propellers, pneumatic actuators for rapid opening and closing of bomb bay doors, and other modifications.[5] Potential targets for the 509th were determined by a special military committee: Kokura, the site of one of Japan's largest munitions plant; Hiroshima, an embarkation port and industrial center that also housed a major military headquarters; Niigata, an industrial port with steel and aluminum manufacturing facilities and an oil refinery; and Kyōto, a major industrial center. By early June, all preparations were complete and the necessary elements flew to North Field on the island of Tinian. The goal was to convince the Japanese to surrender in accordance with the conditions to be set at the upcoming Potsdam Conference.

On July 26, the United States, Great Britain, and China released the Potsdam Declaration, announcing the terms for Japan's surrender, coupled with a warning to the Japanese government to accept the Allied demand for the unconditional surrender of all Japanese armed forces, and to provide adequate assurances of its good faith in taking such an action. The alternative for Japan was its prompt and utter destruction. Prime Minister Suzuki declared that Japan would ignore the declaration, which was interpreted by the Allies as a rejection that reinforced the belief that the Japanese military remained in control of the government and only a decisive act of violence could remove it.

At 0145 on August 6, three weather reconnaissance aircraft launched from Tinian. Headed for Hiroshima was *Straight Flush*, code-named Dimples 85, piloted by Major Claude Eatherly. *Jabit III*, code-named Dimples 71, piloted by Major John Wilson, set a course for Kokura. *Full House*, code-named Dimples 83, piloted by Major Ralph Taylor, plotted a course for Nagasaki. One hour later, three additional aircraft lumbered down North Field and lifted into the night sky. *The Great Artiste*, code-named Dimples 89, piloted by Major Charles Sweeney, *Necessary Evil*, code-named Dimples 91, flown by Captain George Marquardt, and *Enola Gay*, code-named Dimples 82, piloted by Colonel Paul Tibbets, set their navigation instruments toward Japan. While the primary target was Hiroshima, the final decision on which city to bomb would be determined by the three weather reconnaissance aircraft. An uneventful flight did not diminish the significance of their plan. Aboard *Enola Gay* was the first product of the Manhattan Project.

At about 0700, *Straight Flush* flew over the city of Hiroshima and conducted its assigned task of weather reconnaissance, then broadcast a short message indicating that the cloud cover was less than three-tenths of a mile at all altitudes and the primary target would be attacked.[6] Colonel Tibbets started his bomb run at 0809, then turned control over to his bombardier, Major Thomas Ferebee. Six minutes later, the bomb bay doors opened over Japan's eighth largest city and the world's first nuclear bomb, code-named Little Boy, was released at an altitude of just over thirty-one thousand feet. Tibbets resumed control and executed a well-rehearsed diving turn to avoid the effects of the blast. Forty-three second later, Little Boy detonated at an altitude of just over two thousand feet. Tibbets and his crew were just over eleven miles away when they felt the first shock waves. Tibbets later described "the awesome sight that met our eyes as we turned for a heading that would take us alongside the burning, devastated city. The giant purple mushroom, which the tail-gunner had described, had already risen to a height of 45,000 thousand feet, 3 miles above our own altitude, and was still boiling upward like something terribly alive."[7]

President Truman, on board the cruiser USS *Augusta*, a *Northampton*-class heavy cruiser used as a presidential flagship by both Roosevelt and Truman, was on his way back from the Potsdam Conference when he received confirmation by radio that the bombing was successful.

In South Cle Elum, Edith and James, along with neighbors and friends listened later that day as President Truman, in a radio broadcast announced the use of the atomic bomb:[8]

> *Sixteen hours ago an American airplane dropped one bomb on Hiroshima, an important Japanese Army base. That bomb had more power than 20,000 tons of T.N.T. It had more than two thousand times the blast power of the British "Grand Slam" which is the largest bomb ever yet used in the history of warfare.*
>
> *The Japanese began the war from the air at Pearl Harbor. They have been repaid many fold. And the end is not yet. With this bomb we have now added a new and revolutionary increase in destruction to supplement the growing power of our armed forces. In their present form these bombs are now in production and even more powerful forms are in development.*
>
> *It is an atomic bomb. It is a harnessing of the basic power of the universe. The force from which the sun draws its power has been loosed against those who brought war to the Far East.*

Before 1939, it was the accepted belief of scientists that it was theoretically possible to release atomic energy. But no one knew any practical method of doing it. By 1942, however, we knew that the Germans were working feverishly to find a way to add atomic energy to the other engines of war with which they hoped to enslave the world. But they failed. We may be grateful to Providence that the Germans got the V-1's and V-2's late and in limited quantities and even more grateful that they did not get the atomic bomb at all.

The battle of the laboratories held fateful risks for us as well as the battles of the air, land and sea, and we have now won the battle of the laboratories as we have won the other battles . . .

We are now prepared to obliterate more rapidly and completely every productive enterprise the Japanese have above ground in any city. We shall destroy their docks, their factories, and their communications. Let there be no mistake; we shall completely destroy Japan's power to make war.[9]

Many gathered around the radio nodded in agreement, and one individual patted James on the back.[10] The president continued, "It was to spare the Japanese people from utter destruction that the ultimatum of July 26 was issued at Potsdam. Their leaders promptly rejected that ultimatum. If they do not now accept our terms they may expect a rain of ruin from the air, the like of which has never been seen on this earth. Behind this air attack will follow sea and land forces in such numbers and power as they have not yet seen and with the fighting skill of which they are already well aware . . ."[11]

After the president concluded his remarks, most of those in the Munro home were silent as James turned off the radio. Edith and the ladies slowly retired quietly to the kitchen while the men remained seated in the living room. A man seated next to James quipped, "I guess we wait." Those in the room nodded in agreement.[12]

The world was silent and waited for word from the Japanese government. The day after the bombing, Hiroshima was inspected by Japanese atomic physicists who confirmed the use of an atomic weapon. Admiral Soemu Toyoda, chief of the Naval General Staff, argued in a radio message intercepted by American code breakers that the U.S. only had two more such weapons and stated "there would be more destruction but the war would go on."[13]

The following day on the island of Guam, a meeting of Project Alberta leaders was held. Since Japan had given no indication it would surrender, the decision was made to proceed with dropping a second bomb in order to persuade the Japanese that the Allies had, in fact, multiple atomic weapons. Responsibility for scheduling of the second bombing fell to Colonel Tibbets. Due to weather concerns, he selected August 9 and chose Kokura as the primary target. Kokura had been the secondary target for Little Boy on August 6, 1945. If Hiroshima had been clouded over, the first bomb would have been dropped on Kokura.

Two weather reconnaissance aircraft, *Enola Gay*, code-named Dimples 82, flown by Captain George Marquardt, and *Laggin' Dragon*, code-named Dimples 95, piloted by Captain Charles McKnight, took off at 0249. *Enola Gay* plotted its course for Kokura and the *Laggin' Dragon* flew toward Nagasaki. One hour later, Major Charles Sweeney lifted off in *Bockscar*, code-named Dimples 77, loaded with Fat Man, a more potent weapon than the one that had been used over Hiroshima. Accompanying *Bockscar* was *The Great Artiste*, code-named Dimples 77, piloted by Captain Frederick Bock, and *Big Stink*, code-named Dimples 90, flown by Major James Hopkins Jr. With Kokura as the primary target, Nagasaki was plotted as a secondary target. When *Bockscar* reached Kokura, a 70 percent cloud cover obscured the city and Sweeney diverted to Nagasaki. At 1101, *Bockscar*'s bombardier, Captain Kermit Beahan, visually sighted the target and released Fat Man, which detonated just over fifteen hundred feet above the city.[14]

Until August 9, Japan insisted on a conditional surrender; however, after the destruction of Nagasaki, Emperor Hirohito held an imperial conference and authorized Tōgō to notify the Allies that Japan would accept the terms of the Potsdam Declaration. On August 14, Hirohito broadcast his surrender announcement to the Japanese people, in which he stated in part, "Moreover, the enemy now possesses a new and terrible weapon with the power to destroy many innocent lives and do incalculable damage. Should we continue to fight, not only would it result in an ultimate collapse and obliteration of the Japanese nation, but also it would lead to the total extinction of human civilization. Such being the case, how are We to save the millions of Our subjects, or to atone Ourselves before the hallowed spirits of Our Imperial Ancestors? This is the reason why We have ordered the acceptance of the provisions of the Joint Declaration of the Powers."[15]

Early in the morning of August 15, 1945, the Japanese Foreign Ministry sent telegrams to the Allies through the Swiss Federal Political Department that Japan accepted the terms of the Potsdam Declaration. News of the Japanese surrender spread throughout the free world quickly and was celebrated in the streets of Cle Elum. James and Edith received a steady stream of visitors, telephone calls, and telegrams during the following weeks.[16]

General Douglas MacArthur arrived in Tokyo on August 30, and the formal surrender ceremony occurred on September 2, 1945, when representatives from the Empire of Japan signed the Japanese Instrument of Surrender in Tokyo Bay on board the battleship USS *Missouri*. President Truman declared that September 2 would be celebrated as Victory over Japan Day, more popularly known as V-J Day. After the formal surrender, an investigation into Japanese war crimes began quickly.

The Munro family, relatives, and friends again gathered at the Munro home to listen to the formal surrender on the radio. Everyone celebrated the victorious end of the war in Cle Elum, as did most people around the world. The war had ended for Douglas

Munro on September 27, 1942, but for James, Edith, John, and Patricia, it would continue until Douglas returned home.[17]

Military and government officials had begun the planning process for his repatriation and that of all of America's war dead as early as October 1943. With the halt of Japanese expansionism in the South Pacific and the victory at Guadalcanal, the United States had turned the entire outlook of the war. Prudence demanded planning for the postwar repatriation of America's honored fallen. The quartermaster general, as chief of the American Graves Registration Service (AGRS; now known as Mortuary Affairs), acted as the representative for all branches of the armed services and various civilian agencies. An organizational structure consisting of three AGRS area commands, fourteen subordinate zone commands, and assigned field operating units studied the challenges of establishing permanent overseas cemeteries. Developed under the direction of the quartermaster general, the plan consisted of three separate parts: The first was to return the remains of American military and civilian dead from outside the continental United States to this country, and deliver them to the next of kin for private interment or burial in national cemeteries. The second was to acquire land for new national cemeteries and to improve and extend the existing ones in the United States. The third was to draft and submit legislation to Congress to fund the purchase of land to create "a limited number of permanent cemeteries on foreign soil for concentration of the remains of our World War II dead whom the next of kin specifically indicated their desire to remain buried abroad."[18]

By the end of April 1945, it was estimated that there were a total of 165,995 recorded burials of Army personnel, and 25,000 of Navy, Marine Corps, and Coast Guard personnel; 44,243 were reported missing in action. However, two additional and important factors were yet to be determined or proven: First, the number of deaths yet to be sustained in the defeat of the Japanese Empire, and second, the assumption that 90 percent of those reported missing were actually dead and that the remains of 50 percent of the missing would be recovered through systematic search. This resulted in an astonishing assumption that more than three hundred thousand burials would be needed by the end of the war.

Regardless of the enormity of the task, two core values anchored the planning and execution of the AGRS: The American people, especially the families of lost military personnel, deserved the most accurate accounting possible; and all repatriated remains deserved to receive honors consistent with military protocol and tradition. As of April 1946, there were a total of 359 American military cemeteries that served as the resting place for 241,500 fallen American heroes of World War II. Although the number of burials in the Pacific areas totaled less than one-fifth of those in the European and Mediterranean theaters, the wide dispersal of gravesites among the many islands and archipelagoes of the central and southwest Pacific and landmasses of New Guinea and Australia presented complex challenges.[19] In Douglas Munro's case, location and identification were not an issue.

In late October 1947, Edith received a call from the Coast Guard tactfully and professionally asking if the Munros would like the body of their son brought back to the United States. Edith quickly and emotionally answered, "Yes, of course." She was informed that they would receive a visit from both Navy and Coast Guard officials in the very near future.

During the first week of November, Navy and Coast Guard officials arrived and informed the family of the repatriation procedure and offered Arlington National Cemetery as a final resting place for their son. After a few minutes of emotional discussion, the family respectfully declined the offer for burial at Arlington and requested that Douglas be returned to Cle Elum. During the brief meeting, the officers told them they would keep the family fully informed and assured them of the utmost care and respect for their son and all of America's fallen heroes. As the officers drove away, Edith turned and hugged James, saying through her tears, "He's coming home, James. Douglas is coming home." Word of Doug Munro's repatriation spread quickly throughout Cle Elum and the nearby towns of Roslyn and Ellensburg.[20]

James, in addition to his work responsibilities, now had a lot of planning to do, but realized that he was too close to the situation to do so effectively. Over the course of the next several weeks, he purchased a large multiple-grave plot in the Veterans Section of Laurel Hill Cemetery in Cle Elum; he also met with his friend Commander Earl McDonald of the Herbert Irwin Post of the Veterans of Foreign Wars and asked him to handle the details of coordinating with the Navy and Coast Guard Douglas's transfer to Cle Elum, establishing calling hours, and planning military graveside services. James, Edith, and Commander McDonald met with representatives from Coleman Funeral Chapel, but thereafter, Commander McDonald coordinated all of the details and scheduling. James asked another friend and veteran, Thomas Woodward, a lay reader in the Episcopal church, to officiate the graveside military service. An official from the various organizations and the funeral home later met with James and Edith to coordinate the schedule and assure them that all proper military honors would be afforded to their son.[21]

On November 9, the U.S. Army Transport (USAT) *Goucher Victory* arrived at Guadalcanal and disembarked men and equipment. A formidable challenge faced the workers; "over three thousand remains were to be disinterred, processed and casketed within the following sixty-two days during the worst of the rainy season." Additional supplies, including "final-type caskets," arrived on board the USAT *Walter W. Schwenk* on November 13.[22]

Actual exhumations began on November 27 and were completed on December 20, with crews working six days a week. The USAT *Cardinal O'Connell* arrived at Guadalcanal during the third week of December. The master of the ship assumed responsibility for the caskets as they reached the pier and so to it they were honorably placed on board ship before work ceased at any given time.

Both the *Goucher Victory* and the *Cardinal O'Connell* departed Guadalcanal on January 12, 1948; the former steamed for Saipan, while the latter headed for the Navy yard in Honolulu, Hawaii, with 2,792 fallen heroes, including Medal of Honor recipient Douglas A. Munro.[23]

A destroyer escort joined the *Cardinal O'Connell* about twenty miles from port, and as the ships entered Pearl Harbor those on board the destroyer escorts manned the rails. As the *Cardinal O'Connell's* mooring lines were secured midmorning, a joint military band played softly, and numerous transport vehicles lined up with hundreds of men as military escorts and honor guards. Military and political leaders were present as well. American and military unit flags moved quietly in the gentle island breeze under a cobalt blue sky with scattered light clouds. The flag-draped remains of the fallen that were to be interred in the National Memorial Cemetery of the Pacific in Hawaii were carefully transferred to the awaiting transport vehicles by the military honor guards, a process that continued for several days.[24]

After nearly a week in Hawaii, the *Cardinal O'Connell* cast its mooring lines and slowly pulled away from the dock, turned, and headed toward the entrance of Pearl Harbor. Past both Hospital and Bishop's Points and Hickam Field it steamed, through the harbor channel and into the waters of the Pacific, where destroyer escorts moved into position off the port and starboard sides for the solemn two-thousand-mile voyage to San Francisco.

Early in the morning of February 12, the *Cardinal O'Connell* and its destroyer escort entered the three-mile Golden Gate channel between the vast Pacific and San Francisco Bay, passed under the Golden Gate Bridge, completed a hard starboard turn, and proceeded under the San Francisco–Oakland Bay Bridge and moored at the Navy and Coast Guard base at Treasure Island, a four-hundred-acre man-made island in San Francisco Bay. The ship was greeted by a full-service honor guard and a Navy band.[25]

Disembarkation of the flag-draped caskets of the fallen heroes began two days later and proceeded in a solemn and orderly fashion. When the Navy and Coast Guard honor guard brought the casket containing the remains of Douglas Munro ashore, it was immediately placed in a black hearse between a lead and chase car and taken to the railroad station. There, it was loaded onto a catafalque in an empty train car with black curtains accenting the windows and red, white and blue bunting along the outside just below the windows. On the train, the honor guard consisted of four Navy and four Coast Guard personnel. One man took a position at each corner of the flag-draped casket. The other four men served as relief and later as escorts for Edith and Patricia. Immediately behind the funeral car was an empty passenger car. The train departed and began the eight-hundred-mile journey north to the Auburn Army Air Force Base near Seattle, Washington. It arrived late in the morning of March 5.[26]

In Auburn, James, Edith, John, and Patricia boarded the empty passenger car behind the car carrying the remains of their son and brother. They were given several minutes of personal time as the honor guard changed before the train began its final seventy-eight-mile journey to the depot in Cle Elum, located right next to Munro's boyhood home. As the train slowly entered the Cle Elum station, a large contingent of veterans, Boy Scouts, friends, and relatives, most carrying small American flags, had assembled. As the train stopped, the local veterans band began playing soft patriotic music while the honor guard moved the casket from the train to a waiting hearse. As the hearse slowly made its way through town, the streets were lined with men, women, and flag-waving children. After arriving at the Coleman Funeral Chapel, the honor guard transferred the casket into the largest room, already set up with Navy, Coast Guard, American, and Washington State flags along the walls. After the casket was placed on the bier, a large picture of Douglas Munro was positioned near the head of the casket, and a large arrangement of flowers was put at the opposite end. Smaller floor plants and flowers lined the length of the flag-draped casket. A small linen-draped table centered with the casket displayed the Medal of Honor. Several tables displayed family photographs and other memorabilia. The honor guard rotated every thirty minutes: one man at each end of the casket, with the Coast Guard representative at the head.[27]

The family met privately with Captain A. M. Martinson, the chief of staff of the 13th Coast Guard District, and Lieutenant Commander J. B. Muzzy. Although calling hours were not scheduled until the next morning, by early evening, a large gathering of mourners stood silently outside in the brisk cold wind. When Edith and James were told of the growing crowd, Edith turned to James and said, "They are here to honor Douglas. We need to get those people inside and out of this weather." James nodded in agreement and informed Coleman personnel that the family would stay and see everyone. Coleman officials quickly sat up chairs for the family and opened the doors. Over the course of the next three hours, James, Edith, John, and Patricia received family, friends, and other mourners.[28]

At nine o'clock that evening, Coleman officials requested that those in line return at ten the next morning. Having heard the request, Edith again turned to James, who immediately walked over and said something to the official. The doors remained opened until the last visitor had been received. Physically and emotionally exhausted, the family returned home that night just after ten o'clock.[29]

By the time James, Edith, John, and Patricia arrived back at the funeral home the following morning, another large line had formed that extended well down the street. Despite being nearly thirty minutes early, Edith instructed Coleman personnel to open the doors. The family received visitors for another four hours. At about one-thirty in the afternoon, the room was cleared of all visitors. Pallbearers Ray Giaudrone, Alvin Marietta, Bob Nelson, Tony Stoves, Vernon Peterson, and Junior Sandona, all wearing their military uniforms, carried Douglas Munro's flag-draped casket out through the large set of double front doors and down the steps, passing through the large crowd of mourners as the military honor guard snapped to attention. As the lengthy motorcade proceeded down the center of town, the street was lined with people who stood silently. A small crowd gathered at the cemetery entrance, and groups of people stood at various points along the driveway to the gravesite.

As the motorcade arrived, the veterans' honor guard—consisting of Fred Drovetto; Dean Gordanier; Commander Cecil Gaviler of Cle Elum American Legion Post No. 166; Commander Pete Osiadacz of Roslyn-Ronald Legion Post No. 206; Commander Ed Violetta of Robert H. Brooks Veterans of Foreign Wars Post No. 4125; Verne Peterson; Harold Giaudrone; and John Devereaux—stood at the head of the grave. Off to the side were color guards from Boy Scout Troop 84, Doug's old troop, from Cle Elum; Boy Scout Troop 85, also from Cle Elum; Boy Scout Troop 88, from nearby Roslyn; the American Legion; and the Veterans of Foreign Wars. A firing squad consisting of David Haight, Valery Zrebiec, Vic Choyers, H. C. Benjamin, and Jack Lensky as officer of the day stood silently at attention off in the distance. The pallbearers solemnly placed the casket on the lowering device above the grave as a cold wind whipped the colors. Episcopal lay reader Thomas Woodward stepped forward, and, with his words echoing from the snow-covered wooded hills surrounding the cemetery, he recited the Commendation Rites of the Church.[30]

> *Give rest, O Christ, to your servant with your saints, where sorrow and pain are no more, neither sighing, but life everlasting. You only are immortal, the creator and maker of mankind; and we are mortal, formed of the earth, and to earth shall we return. For so did you ordain when you created me, saying, "You are dust, and to dust you shall return." All of us go down to the dust; yet even at the grave we make our song: Alleluia, alleluia, alleluia. Give rest, O Christ, to*

your servant with your saints, where sorrow and pain are no more, neither sighing, but life everlasting.

 Into your hands, O merciful Savior, we commend your servant Douglas Albert Munro. Acknowledge, we humbly beseech you, a sheep of your own fold, a lamb of your own flock, a sinner of your own redeeming. Receive him into the arms of your mercy, into the blessed rest of everlasting peace, and into the glorious company of the saints in light. Amen.[31]

Members of the Navy and Coast Guard honor guard stepped forward and methodically folded the burial flag, which was handed to Lieutenant (junior grade) Frank Ryman of the 13th Coast Guard District, who presented the flag on behalf of the president of the United States and a grateful nation for Douglas's faithful service and ultimate sacrifice in defense of freedom. The firing squad's three-round volley startled Edith and Patricia and echoed through the cemetery. It was followed by the haunting notes of "Taps" from the bugle of Ernie Brensnikar, reminding the Munro family of a much earlier day when Doug performed the same duty for fallen veterans. As the ceremony concluded, Edith and Patricia hugged, James and John shook hands, and Edith and James embraced.

Edith managed a faint smile and said, "He's home."[32]

CHAPTER 10

HONOR, RESPECT, DEVOTION TO DUTY

Mike Cooley returned to Cle Elum shortly after the war and immediately utilized his military-acquired construction skills in the booming post–World War II economy. His work required extensive travel throughout the country for the next decade. He returned to Cle Elum permanently in the late fall of 1958 and quickly became involved in local veterans organizations and joined both the American Legion and the Veterans of Foreign Wars. In a short period of time, he ascended to a position of leadership as a member of the local VFW's House Committee. It was during this time that he learned that Doug Munro had been repatriated, and it wasn't long before he made his first trip to Laurel Hill Cemetery to honor his boyhood friend.[1]

When he arrived at the cemetery, he found the marble military-issued engraved headstone and two deck guns that stood watch over this American hero's gravesite; however, he was disappointed by the tattered and faded flag at the top of the flagpole, which was not illuminated.[2] The deck guns were two MK22 Mod 3-inch .50 calibers. The history of the guns was somewhat vague; one was manufactured in Chicago, Illinois, in 1943, and the other came from Canton, Ohio, in 1942. Originally, the guns were located at City Hall, but on July 12, 1954, the city of Cle Elum agreed to transfer both guns to the Munro gravesite. The flagpole originally stood in front of the Safeway Store on the corner of Thirty-fifth and Roxberry SW in West Seattle. When the store was closed, Senior Chief Yeoman Everest Black, USCG (Ret.), convinced store officials to donate the flagpole to the Cle Elum cemetery.[3] Mike Cooley was able to obtain a new flag from the small stock at the VFW; however, an American flag flying from a nonilluminated flagpole after dusk was unacceptable. Carrying the new flag in a large plastic bucket, he began his twice-daily ritual.[4]

AFTER COMPLETING SERVICE in World War II and earning three battle stars for service in the Korean War, the USS *Douglas Munro* was decommissioned and placed in reserve at Mare Island on June 24, 1960. Mare Island, located twenty-five miles northeast of San Francisco, is the site of the first U.S. Naval Base on the Pacific Ocean. The *Munro* was subsequently struck from the Navy List on December 1, 1965, and in January 1966 it was sunk as a target.

JAMES MUNRO TRANSFERRED to the Renton Substation, located in King County, eleven miles southeast of Seattle; Renton straddles the southeastern shore of Lake Washington at the mouth of the Cedar River ninety minutes northwest of Cle Elum. James and Edith continued to attend Coast Guard events around the country until James's untimely death on Friday, April 13, 1962, at the age of seventy. On Monday, April 16, with full graveside military rights conducted by the Cle Elum American Legion, the VFW, and the Washington State Guard, James was laid to rest in the Munro family plot to his son's right. Edith had lost the two most important men in her life.[5]

Soon after James's death, Edith curtailed her travel and moved to Beaverton, Oregon. On Friday, August 16, 1963, accompanied by a Coast Guard escort, Edith attended the dedication of Munro Hall as the new enlisted barracks and general mess at the Coast Guard Academy in New London, Connecticut. It was her first return visit to the academy since her graduation and subsequent commissioning twenty years earlier.[6]

Without her son and husband, Edith's life centered on her remaining family. She enjoyed living in Helena, Montana, with John and Patricia. At the request of the Coast Guard, at the age of eighty-two, she traveled cross-country to New Orleans escorted by her grandson, Lieutenant (junior grade) Douglas Sheehan, as the honored guest at the September 27, 1971, commissioning of the USCGC *Munro*.[7]

A 378-foot high-endurance cutter (WHEC-724), the *Munro* was the first to be named for a Coast Guard hero. Previous WHECs had been named for secretaries of the treasury, a Coast Guard tradition that dated back to 1830 when the first cutter was named for Alexander Hamilton. Jennie Volpe, wife of Secretary of Transportation John A. Volpe, served as the ship's sponsor. The *Munro* had an original complement of 17 officers and 143 enlisted men; its first commanding officer was Captain John T. Rose. Eight months later, on April 15, 1972, under a cloudless sky, the *Munro* was dedicated at its first homeport of Boston, Massachusetts. However, the ship's stay in Boston was brief.[8]

The needs of the Coast Guard required the reassignment of two cutters to the West Coast. The *Munro* and the *Boutwell* were assigned to their new homeport in Seattle, Washington on Wednesday, August 29, 1973. The *Boutwell* , also a 378-foot high-endurance cutter, was named in honor of George Boutwell, a secretary of the treasury in President Ulysses S. Grant's cabinet. While both ships were enthusiastically welcomed by Seattle residents, the *Munro* quickly became a media and hometown favorite.[9]

IN THE SPRING of 1975, Edith received notification that the large athletic complex on Governors Island, New York, would be renamed in honor of her son in mid-July.[10] Governors Island, a 172-acre island in the Upper New York Bay, approximately one-half mile from the southern tip of Manhattan Island, was the home of the Revolutionary War–era Fort Jay and Castle Williams, and the site of the largest Coast Guard installation and headquarters for the service's regional and Atlantic Ocean operations.

IN 1976, CONGRESS authorized the Veterans Administration to provide specialized military headstones for Medal of Honor recipients. Officials from the Cle Elum VFW post completed the required forms for Edith's signature, and about six weeks later the new gold engraved Medal of Honor headstone arrived and was installed by local veterans, followed by a simple ceremony.[11]

The Washington State Legislature dedicated its Medal of Honor monument on November 7, 1976. In excess of eleven feet tall, the granite obelisk is a full-sized replica of the monument located at the Medal of Honor Grove at Freedoms Foundation at Valley Forge, Pennsylvania. It lists the names of all who have received the nation's highest military award from the State of Washington and is located east of the Winged Victory Monument on the Capitol Campus in Olympia.[12]

In Cle Elum, Mike Cooley had been quietly working to have the name of the local VFW post changed to honor his boyhood friend. His efforts paid off when on September 16, 1980, the post officially changed its name to the Douglas A. Munro Post 1373.[13]

JOHN SHEEHAN WAS working in a large paint facility in Spokane, Washington, when he was involved in an industrial accident that resulted in his developing an aggressive form of pulmonary fibrosis.

Over the next several months, he battled increased shortness of breath, a battle he subsequently lost on July 31, 1982.[14]

ONE WEEK FOLLOWING the death of her son-in-law and just over a year before her own death, Edith was the guest of honor at a ceremony in Winter Haven, Florida, marking the fortieth anniversary of the Guadalcanal invasion on August 7, 1982. Again she was escorted by her grandson, Douglas Sheehan, then a lieutenant commander in the U.S. Coast Guard Reserve. Also attending the event was Rear Admiral Dwight H. Dexter, who was living in nearby Naples, Florida. It was the first time Admiral Dexter and Edith had met.[15] Lieutenant Commander Sheehan picks up the story.

> *Admiral Dexter was a great and humble guy, very easy to talk with. He was very gracious to my grandmother. They had a lengthy and heartfelt conversation. Seeing them talking after all those many years is something I will never forget. Later, I said to him, "Knowing how paperwork driven the military is, and given the fact that you were at a barebones forward operating base, how and where did you find the form to recommend my uncle for the Medal of Honor?" He smiled and shook his head and said, "All I ever did was send that letter to your grandmother. I suspect my yeoman made a copy of it and sent it over to the Marines and they took it from there. I know a copy of the letter is in the file." It was an honor and privilege to have the opportunity to meet him. That event would be my grandmother's final Coast Guard public appearance. I think she realized it and getting to meet and talk with Admiral Dexter made it all that more memorable for her.[16]*

To pay tribute to Douglas Munro's honor, respect, and devotion to duty, the "Douglas Munro March," composed by Lewis J. Buckley, then a lieutenant and the director of the U.S. Coast Guard Band,

Unknown Coast Guardsman visits the grave
of Douglas Munro at Lunga Cemetery on
Guadalcanal. (Courtesy of the Sheehan family)

James and Edith Munro receive their son's Medal
of Honor from President Franklin D. Roosevelt in
the Oval Office. (Courtesy of the Sheehan family)

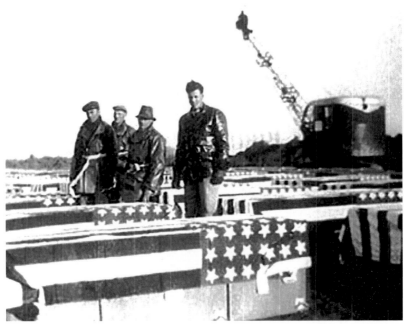

Remains of repatriated servicemen arrive in San Francisco in February 1943. (Courtesy of the Sheehan family)

Funeral ceremony for Douglas Munro after his repatriation, March 6, 1943, at Laurel Hill Cemetery, Cle Elum, Washington. (Courtesy of the Sheehan family)

Medal of Honor headstone of Douglas A. Munro at Laurel Hill Cemetery. (Courtesy of the Sheehan family)

James Munro rests to his son's right. (Courtesy of the Sheehan family)

Edith Munro rests to her son's left. (Courtesy of the Sheehan family)

(Left to right) Master Chief Petty Officer of the Coast Guard Vincent Patton III, Colonel Mac McCloud, Patricia Sheehan, Admiral James Loy, General Terry Drake, assistant commandant of the Marine Corps, and Rear Admiral Douglas Teeson, superintendent of the Coast Guard Academy, at the rededication of Munro Hall at the U.S. Coast Guard Academy. (Courtesy of the Sheehan family)

Munro family headstones at Laurel Hill Cemetery. (Gary Williams)

Panoramic view of the Douglas A. Munro gravesite, designated as a Washington State historical site. (Courtesy of the Sheehan family)

Picture of the larger-than-life statue of Douglas Munro located at the Coast Guard Training Center, Cape May, New Jersey. (Courtesy of the Sheehan family)

Vice Admiral Sally Brice-O'Hara (Ret.), Patricia Sheehan, and Suzanne and Douglas Sheehan at memorial ceremonies at the National Memorial Cemetery of the Pacific, in Hawaii. (Courtesy of the Sheehan family)

Launching of the CGC *Munro*, a Secretary-class 378-foot cutter. (Courtesy of the U.S. Coast Guard)

The WHEC-724 *Munro* is scheduled to be decommissioned when the sixth National Security Cutter is commissioned *Munro* sometime in 2016. (Courtesy of the U.S. Coast Guard)

Memorial stone and plaque located at Honoria, Guadalcanal, near the site of the action that resulted in the death of Douglas Munro and earned him the Medal of Honor. (Courtesy of the Sheehan family)

Memorial plaque donated by the Coast Guard Combat
Veterans Association at the base of the nautical flagpole at the
Douglas Munro gravesite. (Gary Williams)

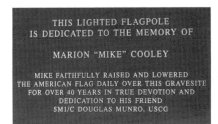

Plaque dedicated to Marion F.
"Mike" Cooley at the base of the
nautical flagpole at the Douglas
Munro gravesite. (Gary Williams)

Major Drew Dix, USA,
Master Sergeant Richard
Pittman, USMC, and
Colonel Jay Vargus,
USMC, all Medal of
Honor recipients, attend
the Medal of Honor
ceremonies aboard the
WHEC-724 *Munro* in
January 2011. (Courtesy
of the U.S. Coast Guard)

Bronze bust with Medal of Honor
located aboard the CGC *Munro*.
(Courtesy of the U.S. Coast Guard)

Medal of Honor recipient "Barney" Barnum, representing the
Congressional Medal of Honor Society and the Marine Corps,
joins then Coast Guard commandant Admiral Robert J. Papp
Jr. at the large bust of Douglas Munro during the dedication of
the new Douglas A. Munro Coast Guard Headquarters building
on November 13, 2013. (Courtesy of the U.S. Coast Guard)

was first performed on September 26, 1982, at the Daughters of the American Revolution Constitution Hall in Washington, D.C.[17]

Having given her only son, and after a long family history of military service in the defense of freedom, Edith Munro died peacefully in her sleep on November 17, 1983, at the age of eighty-eight, and was buried with full military honors. She now rests to her son's left. Her grandson remembers her affectionately as Dede.

"My grandmother was the consummate elegant, refined, well-spoken, and proper British lady," he said, "always focused on service to others and doing the right thing; a characteristic she instilled in her children and grandchildren. Her contributions to our entire family cannot be measured or overstated. My uncle would not have been the man he was; I would not be the man I am today without the love and guidance of my grandmother. She was, quite simply, extraordinary."[18]

Patricia assumed the responsibilities of carrying on the Munro family legacy and attended the dedication of the Douglas Munro statue at Cape May, New Jersey, on September 23, 1986, and subsequently the rededication of Munro Hall at Cape May in May 1989.[19] Commander Douglas James Sheehan, USCGR, retired in 1991, after twenty years of faithful service to his country, having served the last five years in a voluntary no-pay status.[20]

Over the next few years, additional honors continued for the Coast Guard's only Medal of Honor recipient. Coast Guard Station Yankeetown and the Crystal River Order of Eagles dedicated the Douglas Munro Memorial, located in the Little Springs Park just behind City Hall in Crystal River, Florida, on September 27, 1995.[21] However, the Douglas Munro story would soon gain legendary status.

In the spring of 1998, Mike Cooley was in his eighties, his hair now snow white and his complexion pale from a recent bout of pneumonia. His steps were much slower and labored as he shuffled along the three-mile route carrying his five-gallon plastic bucket. Inside was the tattered and faded banner under which he and his boyhood friend fought. Thirty minutes into his journey, he felt the warmth of the sun on his back and saw a few white clouds in the otherwise cobalt blue sky. As the crisp predawn north winds blew down the distant snow-covered Cascade Mountains through the small town, a gust of wind took his breath away, causing him to pause momentarily before continuing on.

Turning onto West First Street, he passed the black iron entrance gates, then looked up and saw his destination, the rust-covered pole in the distance. As he approached, his thoughts were the same this day as always—of his boyhood friend. Several minutes later, he stood in front of the white marble stone with its distinctive gold lettering. He paused, lowered his head in silence, then opened his tear-filled eyes and took a deep breath, looking up at the rusted pole that was in need of replacement. He lacked both the ability and resources to do so, and made temporary repairs as best he could with pieces of rope and small boards.[22]

As he approached the base of the pole, he removed the bucket's precious contents and draped it over his left arm, turned the bucket upside down, and, with his left hand around the pole, stepped up onto the bucket; then, in a reverse figure-eight motion, he removed the lanyard from the cleat. As his hands and knees shook, he secured both the top and bottom brass rings of the banner to the lanyard, and with several quick pulls the national ensign waved in the stiff breeze at the top of the pole. He secured the lanyard to the cleat and stepped down, looked up, and with a shaking hand saluted the flag. He then turned to the right and rendered honors to his friend. Having completed this private ceremony, he began his three-mile journey home. He would return at dusk to strike the flag, a task he had completed without fail yesterday, the day before, and each previous day for the past forty years.

He had made this six-mile round-trip journey twice a day for the past fourteen thousand days and walked some 170,000 miles through sweltering heat, humidity, torrential rains, bitter cold, and wind-driven snow. However, this day was different. His mind troubled. He was concerned about his ability to continue his duty, knowing that a light on the flagpole would alleviate his concern, but he had no resources for such a light. As he walked, he considered his options.[23]

Later that morning, the phone rang in the Coast Guard District Office in Seattle. A staffer in the office answered. The man on the other end of the line said, "My name is Mike Cooley, and I am the post commander of the VFW post in Cle Elum, Washington. I was wondering if the Coast Guard could pay to install a light in the cemetery in Cle Elum at the gravesite of Douglas Munro. If we had a light, then I would not have to raise and lower the flag at the cemetery every day, because the light would shine on the flag. I'm almost eighty-two years old and I won't be able to do this much longer. And after I am gone, I doubt that anyone else will do this."[24]

The Coast Guardsman asked, "How long have you been doing this?"

Cooley calmly responded, "Forty years."

There was prolonged silence in the Coast Guard office. After that call, word spread quickly among the chiefs in the district office, and an article later appeared in the *Seattle Times*. It was only following the article that the Munro family learned of Mike Cooley's honor, respect, and devotion to duty.[25]

What Mike Cooley did not know was that his years of honor, respect, and devotion to duty was about to come to the attention of one of the most influential members of the Coast Guard.

Two thousand miles away in Washington, D.C., Vincent W. Patton III had been sworn in as the eighth master chief petty officer of the Coast Guard (MCPOCG). He was the Coast Guard's top senior enlisted leader and principal adviser to the commandant. Soon after his appointment, he attended a formal military dinner in New York City. Sitting next to him was a Marine Corps corporal who believed Patton to be a master chief in the Navy. Patton corrected him, saying, "No, I am a master chief in the Coast Guard."

The corporal perked up, saying, "The Coast Guard! That's Douglas Munro's service." The corporal then spent the next several minutes telling the story of how Douglas Munro saved the lives of five hundred Marines on Guadalcanal.[26]

When the corporal had finished the story, Master Chief Patton complimented the corporal on his detailed and passionate storytelling, but said, "I have to ask, how do you know that story so well?" The Marine replied, "They teach us that story at Marine Corps boot camp. Douglas Munro saved the lives of Marines, so as far as we are concerned, he is one of us. Besides, the Coast Guard used to be the Revenue Marine . . . and once a Marine, always a Marine."[27]

Patton was astonished that the Marine Corps knew the story of Douglas Munro better than the Coast Guard. It was at that moment that Master Chief Patton determined that he would focus his tenure as MCPOCG on Coast Guard history, heritage, and traditions, including the story of Douglas Munro.[28]

At that time, the Coast Guard's orientation program contained very little about the history and heritage of the service. New courses in Coast Guard history were added at the academy and Training Center Cape May. The honor, respect, and devotion to duty of Petty Officer First Class Douglas Munro were added to the curriculum at both facilities. Patton worked with Master Chief Dave Evans at Cape May to create a museum-quality exhibit to tell the story to all new recruits in Coast Guard boot camp. Within hours after their arrival, new recruits stand around the larger-than-life statue of Douglas Munro and learn his incredible story.[29]

In Seattle, throughout the 13th Coast Guard District which includes the states of Washington, Oregon, Montana, and Idaho, and beyond, the story of Mike Cooley's honor, respect, and devotion to duty spread like a wildfire. Patton picks up the story.

> *The genesis of this project began when an article appeared in the* Seattle Times *. . . This human interest story told of how Mr. Cooley took the long three-mile-walk from his home*

every day to the cemetery to conduct colors honoring his friend and hero. He never missed a day conducting this solemn ritual so that Munro's deed would not disappear. According to his daughter, Mr. Cooley suffered from pneumonia three years ago, yet he still stood the watch twice a day, his daughter had to drive him back and forth, that allowed him to execute his mission, then return home back to bed to convalesce. Mr. Cooley was a truly a remarkable man who was totally committed to keeping his friend's legacy alive, even [if] he had to do it alone.[30]

Patton had distributed the *Seattle Times* article through the CMC (command master chief) network. Within days of the article's distribution, he was inundated with e-mail responses from people throughout the Coast Guard and beyond offering assistance. Patton contacted Master Chief Petty Officer Dave Ojeda, who served as the command master chief (CMC) of the 13th Coast Guard District in Seattle, who in turn reached out to retired Senior Chief Radarman Mark Brown of the Seattle chapter of the Chief Petty Officers Association (CPOA). Master Chief Ojeda and several other chiefs, including Mark Brown, met with Mike Cooley at the cemetery. The consensus of the chiefs was they faced two obstacles: First, a new flagpole was needed; second, there was no source for power to have a lighted flagpole. The chiefs assured Mike Cooley he would soon be formally relieved of his duties.[31]

"No doubt about it," Patton recalled, "this project took on a life of its own, where the true meaning of 'Team Coast Guard' in addition to the D13 chiefs were more than willing to help. The facilities engineer at ISC [Integrated Support Command] Portsmouth [Virginia] offered up the opportunity to get an excess property flagpole that came from Governors Island. However, because the cemetery was not government owned/operated, we had to follow the excess property procedures. There laid an obstacle where another government agency was waiting in the wings to take ownership of it. To a chief, obstacles are merely minor inconveniences which provide opportunities to conquer."[32]

The Yorktown, Virginia, chapter of the Chief Petty Officers Association offered to purchase a new flagpole at the cost of three thousand dollars. The next obstacle was finding someone to install the flagpole, which required permission and assistance from the cemetery. Somebody had to make this happen—especially when the nearest Coast Guard installation was more than eighty miles away. In a matter of days after the project's plan began to materialize, dozens of chiefs from the Seattle area and the entire crew of the Aids to Navigation Team (ANT) based in Kennewick, Washington, drove hundreds of miles over a course of several days in a pilgrimage of sorts to Munro's gravesite. They did this on their own time and at their own expense, surveying the site and visualizing what challenges lay ahead of them. There was no source of power, which had to be installed, with some cooperation and assistance from the local power company. Equipment and supplies had to be obtained to build the foundation of the flagpole. Contractors estimated a cost of sixteen thousand dollars to get power lines from the street to the gravesite twelve hundred feet away. Someone got materials donated, and someone else convinced a local contractor to dig the trench to run the power lines.[33]

During this same time, Cooley also informed the chiefs that the VFW post had been trying for years to erect a memorial veteran's wall that listed the names of servicemen from the State of Washington who had died in past wars. A similar wall did exist at one time attached to the side of a building in the state capital of Olympia, but through neglect in upkeep, the wall was taken down and stored in a warehouse. Cooley and the VFW had made numerous attempts to retrieve it and erect it in the local cemetery. The problem was that the members were elderly and unable to accomplish the work of constructing the wall site. The Seattle CPOA chapter agreed to take on the wall project in conjunction with the flagpole task. Leading the effort was the crew of the ANT Kennewick and the officer in charge, Chief Boatswain's Mate Tom Carroll.

All worked in a concerted effort to ensure that both the wall and the flagpole projects would be completed together. A dedication ceremony was planned for September 27, 1999. Rear Admiral Paul Blayney, who had assumed command of the 13th District the previous August, was scheduled to be the keynote speaker.[34]

After forty years of faithful service to his friend and assured that his dream of a lighted flagpole and veteran's memorial wall were a reality, Mike Cooley died on July 20, 1999. His ashes were buried in the Munro family plot at Laurel Hill just a few feet from his boyhood friend. JoEllen Craig, his daughter, recalled, "None of us had any idea Dad had been going to the cemetery twice a day, every day all those years. I remember taking him a couple of times when he had pneumonia, but none of us ever knew."[35] His children were not the only ones. Although Edith and Patricia knew of Mike Cooley through his involvement in local veterans' organizations, the surviving family members only learned of his commitment after the article in the *Seattle Times*. Doug Sheehan recalled, "Our family was flabbergasted. My grandmother and mother had no idea and neither did I until the article came out. It is only fitting that his final resting place is near my uncle and under the flag he raised and lowered for forty years. Although never formally a member of the Coast Guard, he clearly demonstrated honor, respect, and devotion to duty in a manner most could not believe. Words simply cannot express the depth of my family's gratitude for the commitment Mike Cooley demonstrated not only to my uncle but our entire family and the Coast Guard as a whole."[36]

On Monday, September 27, 1999, the fifty-seventh anniversary of Douglas Munro's death, the lighted flagpole and the veteran's wall were dedicated, according to Patton, "under the clearest sky that the State of Washington had ever seen. I remember someone telling me that the traditional gray skies of western Washington State gave way to a picture perfect day only because Doug Munro and Mike Cooley wanted to make sure they had a perfect view of the action. After all, they're a lot closer to the decision-making process and outcome of that the weather would be."[37]

Patton's office in Washington handled the RSVP list and anticipated anywhere between 150 and 250 attendees, and had four hundred programs printed. On the morning of the event, Patton and other organizers were pleasantly surprised as the number of attendees swelled to well more than 750—some even estimated 800. Patton continued:

> *My quick scan of the crowd displayed a unique diversity that the small town of Cle Elum, with a population of just under twenty-five hundred may have ever experienced before. Attendees came from all over. They came from as far away as St. Petersburg, Florida, Cape Cod, Massachusetts, San Antonio, Texas, Tulsa, Oklahoma, Southern California, to just a few hundred yards across from the cemetery at the nearby Safeway supermarket. The poor town police department of four officers and a dozen volunteers probably witnessed their first traffic congestion since the introduction of the automobile in the town of Cle Elum.*
>
> *There were young schoolchildren, high school students, retirees, and veterans who pulled their uniforms out of the closet after so many years and wore them with pride to this event. There were seaman apprentices to admirals, active, reserve, retired. Even Medal of Honor recipient Air Force colonel Joe Jackson, USAF (retired), was there, wearing his medal around his neck with pride which paved way for the snappiest salutes from everyone. . . . Retired Army sergeant Bill Sumner, a proud Native American decked out in full heritage attire, formed up with the honor guard of chief petty officers who stood by the flags representing every Allied nation that took part in World War II.[38]*

The entire Sheehan family—Pat, Christopher, and Doug and their children—attended the service.[39] Ray Evans also attended but did not wish to speak or be recognized. He did not wear his uniform, stayed obscure, and left immediately after the ceremony. Later, Ray recalled, "It was a wonderful ceremony and a picture-perfect day. I was glad to have had the opportunity to be there, but the ceremony was about Doug, not about me. I did not want to cause any distraction. I was there to honor Doug and his great legacy, not to be honored or recognized. I ask the Coast Guard and Doug [Sheehan] not to make any reference to me or acknowledge my being there and they respected my wishes. It was a great day for my best friend and the entire Coast Guard."[40]

In his keynote remarks, Rear Admiral Blayney paid tribute not only to Douglas Munro, but also honored the selfless service and dedication of his mother. In addition to an impressive Coast Guard contingent, representatives from three Marine Corps units partici-pated: the Henderson Hall Marine Corps installation in Arlington, Virginia; the 1st Marine Division in Okinawa; and the 3rd Ma-rine Division in Japan. In addition to the ceremonies in Cle Elum, several Coast Guard ships, including the *Northland*, a medium-endurance cutter homeported in Virginia, conducted an all-hands ceremony at sea on Georges Bank (east of Nantucket Island), where Douglas Munro's Medal of Honor citation was read, followed by prayer, a moment of silence, the sounding of eight bells, and the playing of "Taps" as the streaming ensign was lowered to the dip.[41]

The Washington State Historical Society subsequently desig-nated Douglas Munro's gravesite a Washington State historical site on January 28, 2000.

CHAPTER 11

COAST GUARD AND MARINE CORPS LEGEND

The National Museum of the Marine Corps opened its doors on November 10, 2006. Located on the museum's Legacy Walk's Wall of Heroes are pictures, accompanied by citations, of the more than two hundred Marines who have received the Medal of Honor since 1863. Unique among the pictures is a portrait of Douglas A. Munro, United States Coast Guard, the only non-Marine so honored.

Patricia Munro Sheehan continued to attend functions at the behest of the Coast Guard to honor and carry on her family's commitment to the Coast Guard and public service until the last two years of her life. Her final public event was the dedication of the USCG Pacific Veterans Memorial at the National Memorial

Cemetery of the Pacific in Honolulu, Hawaii, on January 18, 2008. Surrounded by family, Pat Sheehan passed away peacefully on December 10, 2010, and is at rest in the Munro family plot at Laurel Hill Cemetery in Cle Elum.

With Patricia's death, the honor and responsibility of the Munro legacy passed to her son, Doug. During a memorial gathering at the Sheehan home, Doug recalled that one of his mother's friends approached him and said, "'Do you know how your mother and I became friends? It was through your uncle. One of the many Marines he saved that day was my dad. I was born after he returned. If it had not been for your uncle, I would not be here.' That was a real eye-opener for me. It was one thing to know that your uncle saved five hundred Marines; it's another thing entirely to have a real person stand in front of you as the daughter of one of those Marines. At that moment, it was not just family and Coast Guard history, it was *real*. It was about *real* men, doing extraordinarily *real* things, saving *real* men, and standing before me was a *real* person. I don't think she had any idea how much of an impact that moment had on me. I will never forget it."

Born on July 4, 1947, Douglas James Sheehan was named in honor of his uncle. He and his older brother, Christopher, were raised in Seattle, where they attended elementary school, before the family moved to Kirkland, Washington. In high school, Doug lettered in both basketball and track and graduated at the top of his class of nearly five hundred students. Having received a scholarship, he joined nearly ninety other freshmen at the prestigious Harvey Mudd College. Located in Claremont, California, Harvey Mudd is one of the nation's top liberal arts colleges, well known for its mathematics, science, and engineering programs. Late in his sophomore year, he transferred to Washington State University, where he graduated Phi Beta Kappa with a bachelor of science degree in mathematics in early February 1969.

At the height of the Vietnam War, graduate students were no longer deferred from the draft. Doug decided to enlist rather than wait for his draft notice, but he knew that he had to act quickly. While the Coast Guard seemed like a natural fit, Doug was reticent about going into that branch. "I discussed it with both my mother and grandmother at length. I did not want any special favors. I had nothing but the utmost respect for my uncle and grandmother but I wanted to make my own way." While he requested and received the application for Coast Guard OCS, completing it was a three-day struggle for Doug. "They wanted to me to document any family members or relatives that had served in the Coast Guard and any awards or recognition they had received. I knew if I did that . . ."

At the urging of his grandmother, Doug completed the application noting his uncle's service and Medal of Honor, as well as his grandmother's service. "When I arrived for my OCS interview, I learned that I was one of eighteen hundred candidates for two hundred spots. Just when it seemed like I was 'just another hopeful candidate,' Captain McCann, president of the Interview Board, came out, looked at me, and referred to me as Mr. Munro."

Accepted into OCS, Doug started in Yorktown, Virginia, in late February. "Our first class at OCS was Coast Guard orientation," Doug recalled. "Part of the class was about awards and medals and things like that. The instructor pointed to the giant poster on the wall, of course, the Medal of Honor was at the top. He described each of the awards as well as the criteria, but never mentioned that my uncle had received the Medal of Honor. The focus was on the operation and missions of the Coast Guard, not its history, heritage, and traditions. Being my first day at OCS, I didn't say anything. In fact, the only thing any of my classmates knew about me was my name and where I was from. Having a different last name from my uncle and grandmother helped. I was just trying to make it through the program like everyone else. Anyone who had gone through OCS knows what I am talking about."

Five weeks into OCS, Doug and his classmates received their first day pass.

We didn't know the area and were afraid to go anywhere or do anything that could end up getting us kicked out. So several of us decided to play it safe and visited the Portsmouth Naval Shipyard Museum. When we arrived we noticed a very large exhibit dedicated to my uncle. We started talking to the curator and one thing led to another. One of my classmates asked me, "How do you know so much about this guy?" Without hesitation, I said, "He's my uncle." Well, the cat was out of the bag at that point. We spent a couple of hours there talking. After we got back, it certainly didn't take long for the word to get around. While my classmates thought it was quite a big deal, I can assure you that our instructors did not. I got a sense real quick that while the bar was already high for all of us, for me, the bar was set a little higher, which was great. Right then, I began to embrace the legacy that had been earned with my uncle's life and my grandmother's service. My uncle was my namesake. Like him, I didn't want any special consideration, just the opportunity. They were the best, and I wanted to be just like them.

Following OCS graduation, Ensign Sheehan was assigned to the buoy tender *Ivy* in Astoria, Washington. While in Astoria, he met Suzanne Lindstrom, the sister of one of his boyhood basketball teammates. In February 1972, Doug transferred to Long Beach, California, in charge of port safety and security. That May, he returned to Astoria for his marriage to Suzanne. At the end of his active duty eighteen months later, he reverted to the Coast Guard Reserve and served as the duty officer. Subsequently, he assumed command of the Coast Guard Reserve unit in Everett, Washington. After twenty years of honor, respect, and devotion to duty, Douglas Sheehan retired in 1991 with the rank of commander. Throughout his career, he served as his grandmother's and mother's Coast Guard escort.

HAVING DODGED STORMS and the treacherous waters of the Bering Sea, the crew of the WHEC-724 *Munro*, homeported in Kodiak, Alaska, welcomed Medal of Honor recipients Drew Dix, Jay Vargas, and Richard Pittman on board for a special Medal of Honor replica presentation on January 5, 2011. Doug Sheehan picks up the story.

> *Actor and longtime military advocate Gary Sinise and his LT. Dan Band, along with TRICARE representatives, had been aboard* Munro *sometime in 2010. During the tour of the ship, they noticed only a few dated remembrances of my uncle. They said, "This will never do," and went to work on fixing that. So on January 5, 2011, I was aboard when they dedicated a bronze bust of Douglas Munro, and retired Marine Corps colonel Jay Vargus placed a Medal of Honor replica from the Congressional Medal of Honor Society around the neck, and the entire bust was later encased in Plexiglas. They also donated a very nice portrait and Medal of Honor Citation for the ship that [is] now on the Mess Deck. From what I understand, it was the third visit aboard the* Munro *for Major Dix and TRICARE representatives. Rear Admiral Christopher Colvin, commander of the Seventeenth Coast Guard District, was there. It was a great day to be aboard the* Munro.[1]

It is ironic that sixty-nine years after Douglas Munro was recommended by Marine Corps legend Lewis B. "Chesty" Puller to receive the Medal of Honor, another Marine Corps legend, Jay Vargus, placed the Medal of Honor around the neck of his bust on board the ship that bears his name.

DOUG SHEEHAN AND author Gary Williams connected in February 2011, and on September 27, 2011, both were at Laurel Hill Cemetery, where their collaboration on this World War II story of honor, respect, and devotion to duty started.

POSTSCRIPT

After two months of rapidly declining health, Commander Raymond J. Evans Jr. peacefully crossed the bar on May 30, 2013, at the age of ninety-two. Doug Sheehan remarked, "While it was not unexpected, we were devastated by the loss of Ray. He was the last remaining connection I had to my uncle. He and Dottie had become dear friends of ours. Ray and my uncle will forever be linked to the Coast Guard and Marine Corps on Guadalcanal—the turning point in World War II." Vice Commandant John P. Currier led a Coast Guard contingent of nearly four hundred, as well as a fire team from Marine Corps Security Force Battalion Bangor, during a full honors ceremony for the Coast Guard legend and recipient of the Navy Cross.

As THE DEPARTMENT of Homeland Security neared completion of the new Coast Guard headquarters on the 176-acre site of the former St. Elizabeth's Hospital in southwest Washington, D.C., a bill worked its way through Congress that would further the legacy of Doug Munro. Eleanor Holmes Norton, Washington, D.C.'s congressional delegate, introduced House Resolution (H.R.) 2611, which was cosponsored by Representatives Howard Coble, John Garamendi, and Duncan Hunter. The legislation passed the House on a 411-0 vote on July 17, 2013. The bill then moved to the Senate on July 17, where it subsequently passed. Public Law 113-31 was signed by President Barack Obama on August 9, 2013.

On November 13, 2013, under a bright cobalt blue sky, the United States Coast Guard dedicated the Douglas A. Munro Coast Guard Headquarters Building and unveiled a large bronze bust that is the focal point of the large, window-walled foyer. Representing the Marine Corps at the formal ceremony, legendary Medal of Honor recipient Colonel Harvey "Barney" Barnum succinctly and quite appropriately stated, "Douglas Munro led by example and epitomized the Coast Guard motto *Semper Paratus*, always ready, when he came to the aid of our Marines on Guadalcanal." During the ceremony, Admiral Robert Papp Jr., the commandant of the Coast Guard, said:

> *Our Coast Guard is fortunate to have many great heroes. We have a long history of men and women with the courage to navigate those uncertain and stormy seas that drive others to safe harbor. Douglas Munro was one of those people. . . . His last words, asking about the Marines . . . , "Did they get off?" With his dying breath he thought not of himself, but of those he had gone to rescue. Douglas Munro defines us. He captures perfectly who we are as Coast Guardsmen, and provides a shining example of our Service ethos: I will protect them. I will defend them. I will save them. I am their shield. . . . Too often, when people ask about our Coast Guard, we talk about our missions. And that's important. We do a lot of great things. But if you want someone to know our story, don't tell them* what *we do. Tell them about Douglas Munro and Ray Evans. . . . What defines us as Coast Guardsmen is not what we do, but* who we are *and* how we do it.

The commandant also had an announcement to make. "Douglas Munro and Ray served together almost every day of Doug's career and it is only fitting that they be reunited here in his wonderful headquarters building," he said. "One of the great new features we now enjoy is a modern conference center that is truly a conference center. We will be naming our new conference center the Ray Evans Conference Center in the near future."[1]

True to his word, on February 17, 2014, the filled conference center in the Douglas A. Munro Coast Guard Headquarters Building was formally named the Commander Ray Evans Conference Center. Outside the conference center hangs a large, full-color portrait of Commander Ray Evans and a plaque commemorating both Commander Evans's service and legacy. For the first three years of their careers, Evans and Munro's actions became both Coast Guard and Marine Corps legend. Now their names are linked together again in the first building solely dedicated for use by the Coast Guard. During his remarks at the dedication, Admiral Papp announced that one of the Service's newest fast response cutters would be named for Evans.

During his 2014 State of the Coast Guard address, held in the Ray Evans Conference Center, Admiral Papp announced, "In October we christened our fourth National Security Cutter, the *Hamilton*, which will soon join the *Bertholf*, *Waesche*, and *Stratton*. We will christen our fifth, the *James*, this summer. . . . Our sixth, the *Munro*, is in production . . ." Ray Evans had expressed hope that there would always be "a *Munro* in our fleet," and with Papp's announcement his dream will continue. Little did he know that both he and his shipmate Douglas Munro would be fulfilling the Coast Guard mission and ethos, leading the way for present and future Coast Guardsmen and Guardswomen for at least the next half century.

Semper Paratus.

ACKNOWLEDGMENTS

In two years of research and two years of writing, I have acquired several file boxes of debts to acknowledge. Unfortunately, with a project of this magnitude, any time you begin a list you inevitably and quite unintentionally omit someone. I sincerely hope that this is not the case here.

My sincere thank you to Gunner's Mate Second Class Daniel Cannode, USCG, a Vietnam veteran, for first telling me the incredible story of Douglas Munro, and to Commander Raymond and Dorothy Evans, for their decades of selfless service and sacrifice in defense of freedom. Ray crossed the bar at the age of ninety-two, about a year before this book was published.

This book would not have been possible without the support and assistance of Scott and Christy Mactavish; Randall Fairey; Dr. Robert Browning and Scott Price, Coast Guard Historian's Office; the crews of the Coast Guard cutters *Mellon* and *Yellowfin*; Kelly O'Neill; Cresta Lewis; Robert Ferdon; Darwin Kayner; JoEllen Craig; Brian Cooley; the City of Cle Elum, Washington; Command Master Chief Jason Vanderhaden, 13th District; Vincent

Patton III, 8th Master Chief Petty Officer of the Coast Guard; the Coast Guard Foundation; Angela Hirsch, Coast Guard Public Affairs; MidPointe Library, West Chester, Ohio; Vice Admiral Sally Brice-O'Hara, 27th Vice Commandant of the Coast Guard; the Museum of the Marine Corps; Master Chief Storekeeper William Lindsey; Lieutenant Commander Jeffrey Pile; Sergeant Major Richard Smith, Marine Corps Security Forces BN, Bangor, Washington; Rear Admiral Sandra Stosz and the staff at the Coast Guard Academy; the Seattle Chapter of the Chief Petty Officers Association; Captain Gene Davis, Coast Guard Museum Northwest; Michael Leavitt, 11th Master Chief Petty Officer of the Coast Guard; Tom Metzger, President, Philadelphia Council, Navy League of the United States; the United States Coast Guard; Nadine Santiago; and Ensign Stephen Nolan, USCG.

A special thank you to Harvey "Barney" Barnum Jr., Medal of Honor, Vietnam; Admiral James Loy, 21st Commandant, USCG, and Deputy Secretary, Department of Homeland Security; Lieutenant General James Livingston, USMC, Medal of Honor, Vietnam; Cory Etchberger, Board of Directors, Medal of Honor Grove, Freedoms Foundation at Valley Forge; Admiral Robert J. Papp Jr., 24th Commandant, USCG; and Vice Admiral John P. Currier, 28th Vice Commandant, USCG.

To Commander Douglas Sheehan, USCG (Ret.), nephew of Douglas A. Munro, your wisdom, guidance, and good counsel throughout the last four years have been invaluable. The contacts you initiated, the doors you opened, and the encouragement you provided kept this project moving forward. A most humble and respectful thank you for allowing me the honor and privilege of documenting your uncle's life and legacy. I hope my efforts are worthy of his sacrifice.

Without the love and support of my family and its commodore, command master chief, and executive officer, Tracy, this project simply would not have been possible.

DOUGLAS A. MUNRO'S MEDAL OF HONOR CITATION

The President of the United States in the name of The Congress takes pride in presenting the MEDAL Of HONOR posthumously to

DOUGLAS ALBERT MUNRO, SIGNALMAN FIRST CLASS
UNITED STATES COAST GUARD

Citation:

For extraordinary heroism and conspicuous gallantry in action above and beyond the call of duty as Petty Officer in Charge of a group of 24 Higgins boats, engaged in the evacuation of a battalion of marines trapped by enemy Japanese forces at Point Cruz Guadalcanal, on September 27, 1942. After making preliminary plans for the evacuation of nearly 500 beleaguered marines, Munro, under constant strafing by enemy machineguns on the island, and at great risk of his life, daringly led 5 of his small craft toward the shore. As he closed the beach, he signaled the others to land, and then in order to draw the enemy's fire and protect the heavily loaded boats, he valiantly placed his craft with its 2 small guns as a shield between the beachhead and the Japanese. When the perilous task of evacuation was nearly completed, Munro was instantly killed by enemy fire, but his crew, 2 of whom were wounded, carried on until the last boat had loaded and cleared the beach. By his outstanding leadership, expert planning, and dauntless devotion to duty, he and his courageous comrades undoubtedly saved the lives of many who otherwise would have perished. He gallantly gave his life for his country.

/s/ FRANKLIN D. ROOSEVELT

CITATIONS OF GUADALCANAL MEDAL OF HONOR RECIPIENTS

The President of the United States in the name of The Congress takes pride in presenting the MEDAL OF HONOR posthumously to

MAJOR KENNETH DILLON BAILEY

MARINE CORPS

for service as set forth in the following

Citation:

For The President of the United States of America, in the name of Congress, takes pride in presenting the Medal of Honor (Posthumously) to Major Kenneth Dillon Bailey (MCSN: 0-5100), United States Marine Corps, for extraordinary courage and heroic conduct above and beyond the call of duty as Commanding Officer of Company C, First Marine Raider Battalion, during the enemy Japanese attack on Henderson Field, Guadalcanal, Solomon Islands, on 12 and 13 September 1942. Completely reorganized following the severe engagement of the night before, Major Bailey's company, within an hour after taking its assigned position as reserve battalion between the main line and the coveted airport, was threatened on the right flank by the penetration of the enemy into a gap in the main line. In addition to repulsing this threat, while steadily improving his own desperately held position, he used every weapon at his command to cover the forced withdrawal of the main line before a hammering assault by superior enemy forces. After rendering invaluable service to the battalion commander in stemming the retreat, reorganizing the troops and extending the reverse position to the left, Major Bailey, despite a severe head wound, repeatedly led his troops in fierce hand-to-hand combat for a period of ten hours. His great personal valor while exposed to constant and merciless enemy fire and his indomitable fighting spirit inspired his troops to heights of heroic endeavor which enabled them to repulse the enemy and hold Henderson Field. He gallantly gave his life in the service of his country.

The President of the United States in the name of The Congress takes pride in presenting the MEDAL OF HONOR to
JOHN BASILONE, SERGEANT
UNITED STATES MARINE CORPS
Citation:

For extraordinary heroism and conspicuous gallantry in action against enemy Japanese forces, above and beyond the call of duty, while serving with the 1st Battalion, 7th Marines, 1st Marine Division in the Lunga Area, Guadalcanal, Solomon Islands, on 24 and 25 October 1942. While the enemy was hammering at the Marines' defensive positions, Sgt. Basilone, in charge of 2 sections of heavy machineguns, fought valiantly to check the savage and determined assault. In a fierce frontal attack with the Japanese blasting his guns with grenades and mortar fire, one of Sgt. Basilone's sections, with its guncrews, was put out of action, leaving only 2 men able to carry on. Moving an extra gun into position, he placed it in action, then, under continual fire, repaired another and personally manned it, gallantly holding his line until replacements arrived. A little later, with ammunition critically low and the supply lines cut off, Sgt. Basilone, at great risk of his life and in the face of continued enemy attack, battled his way through hostile lines with urgently needed shells for his gunners, thereby contributing in large measure to the virtual annihilation of a Japanese regiment. His great personal valor and courageous initiative were in keeping with the highest traditions of the U.S. Naval Service.

The President of the United States in the name of The Congress takes pride in presenting the MEDAL OF HONOR posthumously to

HAROLD W. BAUER, LIEUTENANT COLONEL
UNITED STATES MARINE CORPS

Citation:

For extraordinary heroism and conspicuous courage as Squadron Commander of Marine Fighting Squadron 212 in the South Pacific Area during the period 10 May to 14 November 1942. Volunteering to pilot a fighter plane in defense of our positions on Guadalcanal, Lt. Col. Bauer participated in 2 air battles against enemy bombers and fighters outnumbering our force more than 2 to 1, boldly engaged the enemy and destroyed 1 Japanese bomber in the engagement of 28 September and shot down 4 enemy fighter planes in flames on 3 October, leaving a fifth smoking badly. After successfully leading 26 planes on an over-water ferry flight of more than 600 miles on 16 October, Lt. Col. Bauer, while circling to land, sighted a squadron of enemy planes attacking the U.S.S. Mc-Farland. Undaunted by the formidable opposition and with valor above and beyond the call of duty, he engaged the entire squadron and, although alone and his fuel supply nearly exhausted, fought his plane so brilliantly that 4 of the Japanese planes were destroyed before he was forced down by lack of fuel. His intrepid fighting spirit and distinctive ability as a leader and an airman, exemplified in his splendid record of combat achievement, were vital factors in the successful operations in the South Pacific Area.

The President of the United States in the name of The Congress takes pride in presenting the MEDAL OF HONOR posthumously to

DANIEL JUDSON CALLAGHAN, REAR ADMIRAL
UNITED STATES NAVY

Citation:

For extraordinary heroism and conspicuous intrepidity above and beyond the call of duty during action against enemy Japanese forces off Savo Island on the night of 12–13 November 1942. Although out-balanced in strength and numbers by a desperate and determined enemy, Rear Adm. Callaghan, with ingenious tactical skill and superb coordination of the units under his command, led his forces into battle against tremendous odds, thereby contributing decisively to the rout of a powerful invasion fleet, and to the consequent frustration of a formidable Japanese offensive. While faithfully directing close-range operations in the face of furious bombardment by superior enemy fire power, he was killed on the bridge of his flagship. His courageous initiative, inspiring leadership, and judicious foresight in a crisis of grave responsibility were in keeping with the finest traditions of the U.S. Naval Service. He gallantly gave his life in the defense of his country.

The President of the United States in the name of The Congress takes pride in presenting the MEDAL OF HONOR to
ANTHONY CASAMENTO, CORPORAL
UNITED STATES MARINE CORPS
Citation:

For conspicuous gallantry and intrepidity at the risk of his life above and beyond the call of duty while serving with Company D, 1st Battalion, 5th Marines, 1st Marine Division on Guadalcanal, British Solomon Islands, in action against the enemy Japanese forces on 1 November 1942. Serving as a leader of a machine gun section, Corporal Casamento directed his unit to advance along a ridge near the Matanikau River where they engaged the enemy. He positioned his section to provide covering fire for two flanking units and to provide direct support for the main force of his company which was behind him. During the course of this engagement, all members of his section were either killed or severely wounded and he himself suffered multiple, grievous wounds. Nonetheless, Corporal Casamento continued to provide critical supporting fire for the attack and in defense of his position. Following the loss of all effective personnel, he set up, loaded, and manned his unit's machine gun tenaciously holding the enemy forces at bay. Corporal Casamento single-handedly engaged and destroyed one machine gun emplacement to his front and took under fire the other emplacement on the flank. Despite the heat and ferocity of the engagement, he continued to man his weapon and repeatedly repulsed multiple assaults by the enemy forces, thereby protecting the flanks of the adjoining companies and holding his position until the arrival of his main attacking force. Corporal Casamento's courageous fighting spirit, heroic conduct, and unwavering dedication to duty reflected great credit upon himself and were in keeping with the highest traditions of the Marine Corps and the United States Naval Service.

The President of the United States in the name of The Congress takes pride in presenting the MEDAL OF HONOR to
CHARLES W. DAVIS, MAJOR
UNITED STATES ARMY

Citation:

For distinguishing himself conspicuously by gallantry and intrepidity at the risk of his life above and beyond the call of duty in action with the enemy on Guadalcanal Island. On 12 January 1943, Maj. Davis (then Capt.), executive officer of an infantry battalion, volunteered to carry instructions to the leading companies of his battalion which had been caught in crossfire from Japanese machineguns. With complete disregard for his own safety, he made his way to the trapped units, delivered the instructions, supervised their execution, and remained overnight in this exposed position. On the following day, Maj. Davis again volunteered to lead an assault on the Japanese position which was holding up the advance. When his rifle jammed at its first shot, he drew his pistol and, waving his men on, led the assault over the top of the hill. Electrified by this action, another body of soldiers followed and seized the hill. The capture of this position broke Japanese resistance and the battalion was then able to proceed and secure the corps objective. The courage and leadership displayed by Maj. Davis inspired the entire battalion and unquestionably led to the success of its attack.

The President of the United States in the name of The Congress
takes pride in presenting the MEDAL OF HONOR to
MERRITT AUSTIN EDSON, COLONEL
UNITED STATES MARINE CORPS

Citation:

For extraordinary heroism and conspicuous intrepidity above and
beyond the call of duty as Commanding Officer of the 1st Marine
Raider Battalion, with Parachute Battalion attached, during action
against enemy Japanese forces in the Solomon Islands on the night
of 13–14 September 1942. After the airfield on Guadalcanal had
been seized from the enemy on 8 August, Col. Edson, with a force
of 800 men, was assigned to the occupation and defense of a ridge
dominating the jungle on either side of the airport. Facing a formidable Japanese attack which, augmented by infiltration, had crashed
through our front lines, he, by skillful handling of his troops, successfully withdrew his forward units to a reserve line with minimum
casualties. When the enemy, in a subsequent series of violent assaults,
engaged our force in desperate hand-to-hand combat with bayonets,
rifles, pistols, grenades, and knives, Col. Edson, although continuously exposed to hostile fire throughout the night, personally directed defense of the reserve position against a fanatical foe of greatly
superior numbers. By his astute leadership and gallant devotion to
duty, he enabled his men, despite severe losses, to cling tenaciously
to their position on the vital ridge, thereby retaining command not
only of the Guadalcanal airfield, but also of the 1st Division's entire
offensive installations in the surrounding area.

The President of the United States in the name of The Congress takes pride in presenting the MEDAL OF HONOR to
JOSEPH JACOB FOSS, CAPTAIN
UNITED STATES MARINE CORPS
Citation:
For outstanding heroism and courage above and beyond the call of duty as executive officer of Marine Fighting Squadron 121, 1st Marine Aircraft Wing, at Guadalcanal. Engaging in almost daily combat with the enemy from 9 October to 19 November 1942, Capt. Foss personally shot down 23 Japanese planes and damaged others so severely that their destruction was extremely probable. In addition, during this period, he successfully led a large number of escort missions, skillfully covering reconnaissance, bombing, and photographic planes as well as surface craft. On 15 January 1943, he added 3 more enemy planes to his already brilliant successes for a record of aerial combat achievement unsurpassed in this war. Boldly searching out an approaching enemy force on 25 January, Capt. Foss led his 8 F-4F Marine planes and 4 Army P-38's into action and, undaunted by tremendously superior numbers, intercepted and struck with such force that 4 Japanese fighters were shot down and the bombers were turned back without releasing a single bomb. His remarkable flying skill, inspiring leadership, and indomitable fighting spirit were distinctive factors in the defense of strategic American positions on Guadalcanal.

The President of the United States in the name of The Congress takes pride in presenting the MEDAL OF HONOR posthumously to

WILLIAM G. FOURNIER, SERGEANT
UNITED STATES ARMY

Citation:

For gallantry and intrepidity above and beyond the call of duty. As leader of a machinegun section charged with the protection of other battalion units, his group was attacked by a superior number of Japanese, his gunner killed, his assistant gunner wounded, and an adjoining guncrew put out of action. Ordered to withdraw from this hazardous position, Sgt. Fournier refused to retire but rushed forward to the idle gun and, with the aid of another soldier who joined him, held up the machinegun by the tripod to increase its field action. They opened fire and inflicted heavy casualties upon the enemy. While so engaged both these gallant soldiers were killed, but their sturdy defensive was a decisive factor in the following success of the attacking battalion.

The President of the United States in the name of The Congress takes pride in presenting the MEDAL OF HONOR posthumously to

LEWIS R. HALL, TECHNICIAN FIFTH GRADE
UNITED STATES ARMY

Citation:

For gallantry and intrepidity above and beyond the call of duty. As leader of a machinegun squad charged with the protection of other battalion units, his group was attacked by a superior number of Japanese, his gunner killed, his assistant gunner wounded, and an adjoining guncrew put out of action. Ordered to withdraw from his hazardous position, he refused to retire but rushed forward to the idle gun and with the aid of another soldier who joined him and held up the machinegun by the tripod to increase its field of action he opened fire and inflicted heavy casualties upon the enemy. While so engaged both these gallant soldiers were killed, but their sturdy defense was a decisive factor in the following success of the attacking battalion.

The President of the United States in the name of The Congress takes pride in presenting the MEDAL OF HONOR to

MITCHELL PAIGE, PLATOON SERGEANT

UNITED STATES MARINE CORPS

Citation:

For extraordinary heroism and conspicuous gallantry in action above and beyond the call of duty while serving with a company of marines in combat against enemy Japanese forces in the Solomon Islands on 26 October 1942. When the enemy broke through the line directly in front of his position, P/Sgt. Paige, commanding a machinegun section with fearless determination, continued to direct the fire of his gunners until all his men were either killed or wounded. Alone, against the deadly hail of Japanese shells, he fought with his gun and when it was destroyed, took over another, moving from gun to gun, never ceasing his withering fire against the advancing hordes until reinforcements finally arrived. Then, forming a new line, he dauntlessly and aggressively led a bayonet charge, driving the enemy back and preventing a breakthrough in our lines. His great personal valor and unyielding devotion to duty were in keeping with the highest traditions of the U.S. Naval Service.

The President of the United States in the name of The Congress takes pride in presenting the MEDAL OF HONOR posthumously to

NORMAN SCOTT, REAR ADMIRAL
UNITED STATES NAVY

Citation:

For extraordinary heroism and conspicuous intrepidity above and beyond the call of duty during action against enemy Japanese forces off Savo Island on the night of 11–12 October and again on the night of 12–13 November 1942. In the earlier action, intercepting a Japanese Task Force intent upon storming our island positions and landing reinforcements at Guadalcanal, Rear Adm. Scott, with courageous skill and superb coordination of the units under his command, destroyed 8 hostile vessels and put the others to flight. Again challenged, a month later, by the return of a stubborn and persistent foe, he led his force into a desperate battle against tremendous odds, directing close-range operations against the invading enemy until he himself was killed in the furious bombardment by their superior firepower. On each of these occasions his dauntless initiative, inspiring leadership and judicious foresight in a crisis of grave responsibility contributed decisively to the rout of a powerful invasion fleet and to the consequent frustration of a formidable Japanese offensive. He gallantly gave his life in the service of his country.

THE UNITED STATES NAVY AT GUADALCANAL: OPERATION WATCHTOWER, AUGUST 1942

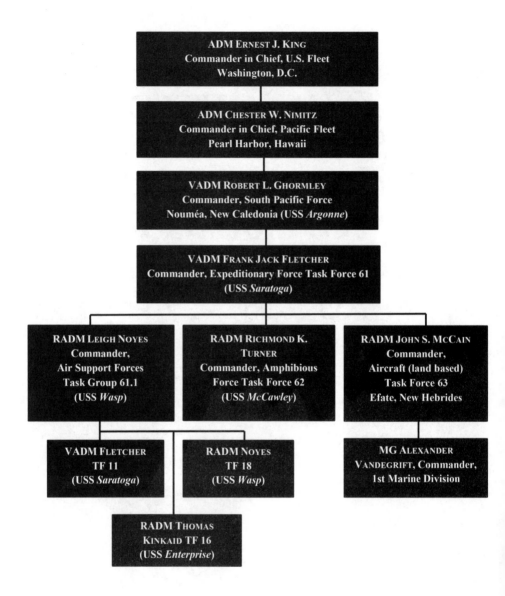

APPENDIX D

SECURITY FOR GUADALCANAL, AUGUST 8–9, 1942

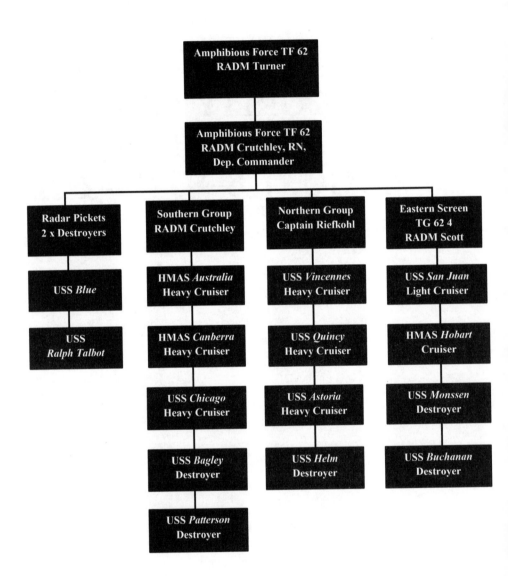

NAVAL BATTLES OF THE GUADALCANAL CAMPAIGN

THE BATTLE OF SAVO ISLAND
AUGUST 8–9, 1942

On August 7, 1942, elements of the 1st Marine Division landed on the beaches of Tulagi and Guadalcanal islands, inflicting heavy casualties on the Japanese. Those not killed were driven deep into the jungle. At the major Japanese base at Rabaul, nearly six hundred miles to the northwest, the newly appointed commander of the Japanese Eighth Fleet, Vice Admiral Gunichi Mikawa, quickly gathered every warship available and steamed toward Guadalcanal. To disrupt the Allied landings, Mikawa's seven cruisers and single destroyer traveled through the New Georgia Sound, also known as "the Slot," and arrived just off of Savo Island in the early morning hours of August 9.

The Allied force consisted of eight cruisers and fifteen destroyers; however, the crews were exhausted from two days of continuous combat and several commanders were away from their ships, setting the stage for the most humiliating defeat in U.S. Navy history. Mikawa guided his ships unseen past the destroyer pickets at the mouth of the sound toward two Allied heavy cruisers, the HMAS *Canberra* and the USS *Chicago*, and two destroyers, the USS *Ralph Talbot* and the USS *Patterson*. The Japanese launched torpedoes and quickly followed with effective fire from their 6- and 8-inch guns. The *Canberra* was immediately sunk, and the *Chicago* was rendered ineffective; the *Ralph Talbot* and the *Patterson* were damaged. Several minutes later, Mikawa split his forces, and the remaining Allied ships were caught in a devastating crossfire; the heavy cruisers *Vincennes*, *Quincy*, and *Astoria* were sunk. Mikawa, unaware that Vice Admiral Fletcher had withdrawn his carriers, decided to pull back through the Slot, which deprived the Japanese of even a greater tactical victory.

THE BATTLE OF CAPE ESPERANCE
OCTOBER 11–12, 1942

On the night of October 11, the Japanese sent a major supply and reinforcement convoy to their forces on Guadalcanal. The Japanese forces included three cruisers, six destroyers, and two seaplane tenders. Shortly before midnight, a U.S force of four cruisers and five destroyers, under the command of Rear Admiral Norman Scott, intercepted the Japanese task force as it approached Savo Island. Taking the Japanese by surprise, the Allied warships sank one cruiser and one destroyer, heavily damaged another cruiser, and forced the rest of the enemy warships to abandon the bombardment mission and retreat. During the exchange of gunfire, the destroyer USS *Duncan* was sunk. The cruiser USS *Boise* and the destroyer USS *Farenholt* were heavily damaged. As with the first naval engagement, the strategic significance was inconsequential because neither the Japanese nor the Americans secured operational control of the waters around Guadalcanal as a result of the action; however, the battle provided a significant morale boost to the U.S. Navy after the disaster at Savo Island.

THE FIRST NAVAL BATTLE OF GUADALCANAL
NOVEMBER 13, 1942

As a result of the bitter fighting on Guadalcanal and surrounding islands, by early November, the Japanese had come to the realization that the Americans had many more troops on the island than had been previously thought, and that if they had any hopes of retaking it, Henderson Field had to be neutralized. On November 11, the Japanese again gathered a large convoy of vessels loaded with supplies for their beleaguered troops on Guadalcanal. To help ensure their safe arrival, two Japanese battleships were to bombard Henderson Field into submission. Just after midnight on the twelfth, in heavy rain squalls, the Japanese entered Iron Bottom Sound. Waiting for them were the light and heavy cruisers and the destroyers of the American force under the command of Rear Admiral Daniel Callaghan.

Due to a series of tactical miscalculations, the resultant battle occurred at point-blank range, with both forces passing through each other's formations. Both sides suffered severe damage, but the Japanese attempt to bombard Henderson Field was thwarted. The Japanese lost three ships, and three more were heavily damaged. On the American side, the light cruiser *Atlanta* and the destroyers *Barton, Cushing, Laffey,* and *Monssen* were sunk; the heavy cruisers *Portland* and *San Francisco*, the light cruisers *Helena* and *Juneau*, and the destroyer *Aaron Ward* suffered heavy damage. The stage was set for a subsequent battle only a day later.

THE SECOND NAVAL BATTLE OF GUADALCANAL NOVEMBER 14–15, 1942

Despite the Japanese losses during the first battle, Admiral Halsey believed that the Japanese would make another run at Henderson Field. Under the command of Rear Admiral Willis Lee, the fast battleships *South Dakota* and *Washington* and destroyers *Preston, Walke, Benham,* and *Gwin* were dispatched to counter the anticipated Japanese attack. The Japanese force of one battleship, one light cruiser, and nine destroyers arrived just off Savo Island. During the battle, the Japanese lost its battleship and a destroyer; the Americans lost the destroyers *Preston, Walke,* and *Benham* and suffered damage to the *South Dakota* and *Gwin*. However, the Americans won the battle and dashed all hopes the Japanese had of retaking Guadalcanal. After this, the momentum of the conflict shifted, with the Japanese playing defense for the rest of the war.

THE BATTLE OF TASSAFARONGA
NOVEMBER 30, 1942

Although the Japanese had made the decision to abandon Guadalcanal, their forces on that island still needed resupply. Loaded with supply drums, Japanese Rear Admiral Raizo Tanaka led eight destroyers down the Slot. Only Tanaka's flagship was fully combat ready. Waiting in Iron Bottom Sound was a U.S. force of four heavy cruisers, a light cruiser, and six destroyers. However, on this night Tanaka's lookouts were very sharp and recognized the ambush before it happened. The Japanese tactic of firing their torpedoes and steaming back through the sound proved effective. The heavy cruiser *Northampton* was sunk and the *Minneapolis*, the *New Orleans*, and the *Pensacola* were heavily damaged, compared to one destroyer lost by the Japanese. While the engagement was a defeat for the U.S. Navy, Japan had begun its withdrawal from Guadalcanal.

APPENDIX F

MAPS

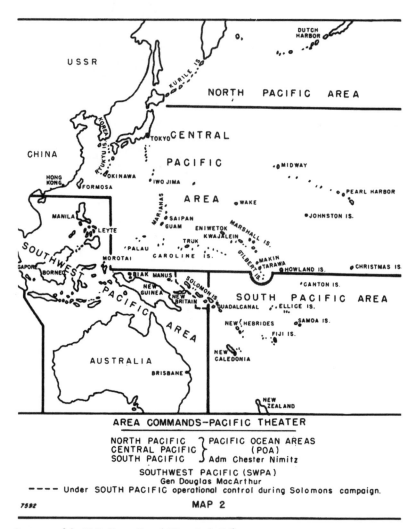

AREA COMMANDS-PACIFIC THEATER

NORTH PACIFIC ⎫ PACIFIC OCEAN AREAS
CENTRAL PACIFIC ⎬ (POA)
SOUTH PACIFIC ⎭ Adm Chester Nimitz
SOUTHWEST PACIFIC (SWPA)
Gen Douglas MacArthur
– – – – Under SOUTH PACIFIC operational control during Solomons campaign.

7592   MAP 2

Courtesy of the U.S. Coast Guard Historian's Office.

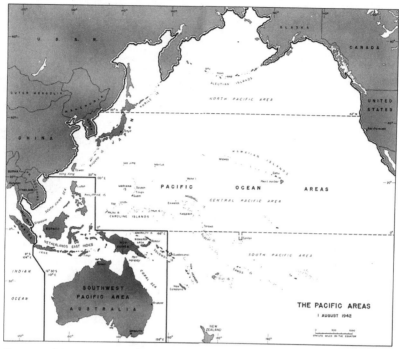

Courtesy of the U.S. Coast Guard Historian's Office.

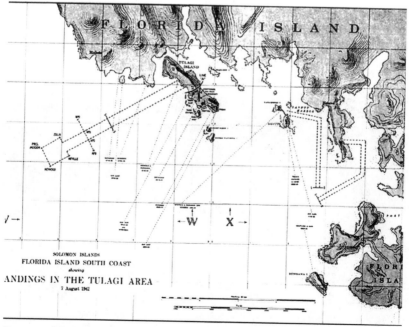

Courtesy of the U.S. Coast Guard Historian's Office.

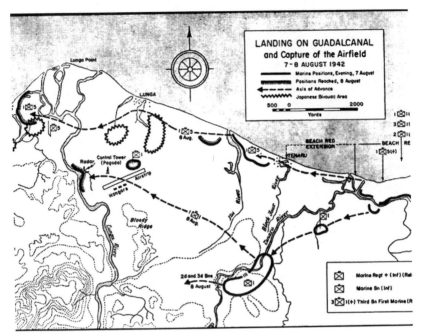

Courtesy of the U.S. Coast Guard Historian's Office.

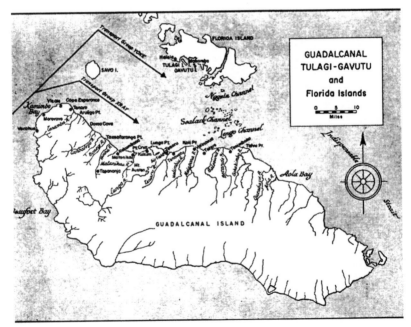

Courtesy of the U.S. Coast Guard Historian's Office.

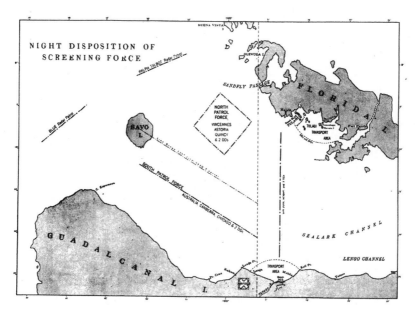

Courtesy of the U.S. Coast Guard Historian's Office.

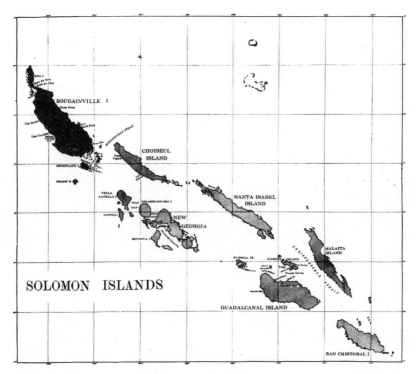

Courtesy of the U.S. Coast Guard Historian's Office.

CREED OF THE UNITED STATES COAST GUARDSMAN

Written by Vice Admiral Harry G. Hamlet, USCG

I am proud to be a United States Coast Guardsman.

I revere that long line of expert seamen who by their devotion to duty and sacrifice of self have made it possible for me to be a member of a service honored and respected, in peace and in war, throughout the world.

I never, by word or deed, will bring reproach upon the fair name of my service, nor permit others to do so unchallenged.

I will cheerfully and willingly obey all lawful orders.

I will always be on time to relieve, and shall endeavor to do more, rather than less, than my share.

I will always be at my station, alert and attending to my duties.

I shall, so far as I am able, bring to my seniors solutions, not problems.

I shall live joyously, but always with due regard for the rights and privileges of others.

I shall endeavor to be a model citizen in the community in which I live.

I shall sell life dearly to an enemy of my country, but give it freely to rescue those in peril.

With God's help, I shall endeavor to be one of His noblest Works . . .

A UNITED STATES COAST GUARDSMAN.

Appendix H

"The Guardian Ethos"

I am America's Maritime Guardian.
I serve the citizens of the United States.
I will protect them.
I will defend them.
I will save them.
I am their Shield.
For them I am *Semper Paratus*.
I live the Coast Guard Core Values.
I am a Guardian.
We are the United States Coast Guard.

UNITED STATES COAST GUARD CORE VALUES

HONOR

Integrity is our standard. We demonstrate uncompromising ethical conduct and moral behavior in all of our personal actions. We are loyal and accountable to the public trust.

RESPECT

We value our diverse work force. We treat each other with fairness, dignity, and compassion. We encourage individual opportunity and growth. We encourage creativity through empowerment. We work as a team.

DEVOTION TO DUTY

We are professionals, military and civilian, who seek responsibility, accept accountability, and are committed to the successful achievement of our organizational goals. We exist to serve. We serve with pride.

NOTES

The research for this narrative was both extensive and wide ranging. Numerous personal and telephone interviews were conducted with Douglas Sheehan, Douglas Munro's nephew, and Munro's friend and shipmate Ray Evans. In addition, the ancestral records of the Munro and Thrower-Fairey families were reviewed in depth. The narrative in chapter 2 is a blend of Munro family oral history, ancestral records, newspaper articles, personal papers, military records, and interviews.

Given the significant loss of leadership, ships, and men, as well as the lack of rations and supplies, during the first major offensive of the war in the Pacific, it is not surprising that official record keeping, from a historical standpoint, was significantly lacking. In many cases, "unofficial" sources such as personal recollection, correspondence, diaries, and logbooks were more detailed, more accurate, or provided the only record of particular events. Due to the incomplete records from the offensive at Guadalcanal, where a conflict existed between official and unofficial sources, I followed the more detailed and accurate unofficial source.

All interviews were conducted by the author, except where noted otherwise. As there were numerous personal and telephone interviews with Ray Evans and over fifty personal and telephone interviews with Douglas Sheehan, citations of these interviews are not dated. All other personal interviews are cited and dated.

Preface

1. *U.S. Coast Guard: A Historical Overview*, 12.

2. Douglas A. Munro Medal of Honor Citation.

Introduction

1. Evans interview.

Chapter 1. Why?

1. Sheehan remarks.

Chapter 2. "Mother, Are You OK?"

1. Cooley interview.

2. Munro family oral history.

3. Sheehan interview; Munro family papers.

4. Munro family papers.

5. Sheehan interview.

6. Borleske, "Overview of the Milwaukee Road Site."

7. Munro family history.

8. Sheehan interview.

9. Ibid.

10. Munro family papers.

11. Ibid.

12. Ibid.

13. Ibid.

14. Ibid.

15. Ibid.

16. Ibid.

17. Ibid.

18. Ibid.

19. Ibid.

20. Ibid.

21. Ibid.

22. Ibid.

23. Ibid.

24. Evans interview.

25. Ibid.

26. Ibid.

27. Ibid.

28. Ibid.

29. Ibid.

30. Ibid.

31. Ibid.

32. Ibid.

33. Ibid.

34. Ibid.

35. Ibid.

Chapter 3. The North Atlantic

1. Evans interview.

2. *U.S. Coast Guard Cutter History, Spencer*, 15.

3. Ibid.

4. Ibid.

5. Ibid.

6. Ibid.

7. Evans interview.

8. White, *Bitter* Ocean, 29.

9. Evans interview.

10. Ibid.

11. Ibid.

12. Ibid.

13. Ibid.

14. Ibid.

15. Ibid.

16. Ibid.

17. Ibid.

18. Munro family oral history.

19. White, *Bitter Ocean*, 29–30.

20. Walling, *Bloodstained Sea*, 4.

21. Ibid.

22. Evans interview.

23. Ibid.

24. Ibid.

25. Ibid.

26. The Maginot Line was a series of concrete formations, obstacles, and weapons installations constructed by France along its border with Germany during the 1930s. It was built in response to France's experience in World War I. A similar line of defenses, the Alpine Line, faced Italy.

27. Known as *Untermehmen Seelöwe*, or Operation Sea Lion, the invasion was postponed indefinitely on September 17, 1940, and never carried out.

28. Evans interview.

29. Munro family oral history.

30. Roosevelt, *Call to Battle Stations*.

31. Evans interview.

32. Munro family oral history.

33. Evans interview.

34. Ibid.

35. Adams, *Ocean Station*, 2.

36. Ibid.

37. Ibid.

38. Evans interview.

39. Ibid.

40. Ibid.

41. Ibid.

42. Munro family oral history.

43. Ibid.

44. Ibid.

45. Ibid.

46. Ibid.

47. Evans interview.

48. Ibid.

49. Ibid.

50. Ibid.

51. During this battle, an Allied force consisting of British Royal Navy and Royal Australian Navy vessels sank or severely damaged several ships of the Italian Regia Marina, giving the Allies control of the Mediterranean Sea.

52. Walling, *Bloodstained Sea*, 12.

53. Ostrom, *United States Coast Guard*, 37.

54. Roosevelt, *Call to Battle Stations*.

55. The Two-Ocean Navy Act, also known as the Vinson-Walsh Act, enacted on July 19, 1940, was the largest naval procurement bill in U.S. history, increasing the size of the Navy by 70 percent. It authorized the construction of 18 aircraft carriers; 2 *Iowa*-class battleships; 5 *Montana*-class battleships; 6 *Alaska*-class cruisers; 27 cruisers of other classes; 115 destroyers; 43 submarines; and 15,000 aircraft. The act also permitted for the conversion of 100,000 tons of auxiliary ships. In addition, it provided $50 million for patrol, escort, and other vessels; $150 million for equipment and facilities; $65 million for ordnance, munitions, and matériel; and $35 million for facility expansion.

56. Evans interview.

57. Ibid.

58. Ibid.

59. Ibid.

60. Kimball, "U.S. Coast Guard at Camp Lejeune," 2.

61. Ibid., 3.

62. Evans interview.

63. Munro family oral history.

64. Evans interview.

65. Ibid.

66. Borneman, *Admirals*, 204.

67. Evans interview.

68. Ibid.

69. Ostrom, *United States Coast Guard*, 22.

70. Evans interview.

71. Ostrom, *United States Coast Guard*, 22.

72. Ibid.

73. Ibid.

74. Ibid.

Chapter 4. The South Pacific

1. Evans interview.
2. Ibid.
3. *Guadalcanal: The U.S. Army Campaign*, 1.
4. Ibid.
5. Leckie, *Challenge for the Pacific*, 1.
6. Ibid., 4.
7. Ibid.
8. Ibid.
9. Ibid.
10. Ibid.
11. Ibid.
12. *Guadalcanal: The U.S. Army Campaign*, 1.
13. Ibid.
14. Leckie, *Challenge for the Pacific*, 12.
15. Ibid.
16. Ibid., 10.
17. Ibid., 3.
18. Hornfischer, *Neptune's Inferno*, 4.
19. Evans interview.
20. Ibid.
21. Ibid.
22. Tregaskis, *Guadalcanal Diary*, 8.

Chapter 5. Operation Watchtower

1. Evans interview
2. Ibid.
3. Hornfischer, *Neptune's Inferno*, 32.
4. Ibid., 34.
5. Ibid.

6. Ibid.

7. Evans interview.

8. Ibid.

9. Ibid.

10. Ibid.

11. Ibid.

12. Ibid.

13. *Landing in the Solomons,* 19.

14. Ibid., 20.

15. Ibid., 27.

16. Ibid., 29.

17. Ibid.

18. Ibid.

19. Ibid., 40.

20. Ibid., 40–41.

21. Evans interview.

22. Ibid.

23. Ibid.

24. Ibid.

25. Ibid.

26. Ibid.

Chapter 6. Naval Operating Base Cactus

1. Leckie, *Challenge for the Pacific,* 87.

2. Brady, *Hero of the Pacific,* 19.

3. Ibid.

4. Frank, *Guadalcanal,* 62.

5. Evans interview.

6. Leckie, *Challenge for the Pacific,* 87.

7. Evans interview.

8. Ibid.

9. *Landing in the Solomons*, 54.

10. Evans interview.

11. *Landing in the Solomons*, 54.

12. Leckie, *Challenge for the Pacific*, 92.

13. Ibid.

14. Newcomb, *Savo*, 92.

15. Ibid.

16. Evans interview.

17. Ibid.

18. Ibid.

19. Ibid.

20. Leckie, *Challenge for the Pacific*, 99.

21. Ibid.

22. Ibid.

23. Ibid.

24. Griffith, *Battle for Guadalcanal*, 67.

25. Evans interview.

26. Ibid.

27. Ibid.

28. Griffith, *Battle for Guadalcanal*, 67.

29. Miller, *Earned in Blood*, 81.

30. Ibid.

31. Leckie, *Challenge for the Pacific*, 191, 192.

32. Ibid., 112.

Chapter 7. "Did They Get Off?"

1. Hough, *Pearl Harbor to Guadalcanal*, 312.

2. Ibid., 313.

3. Ibid.

4. Hurlbut, untitled clipping.
5. Ibid.
6. Ibid.
7. Hoffman, *Chesty*, 172.
8. Hough, *Pearl Harbor to Guadalcanal*, 315.
9. Leckie, *Challenge for the Pacific*, 201.
10. Hough, *Pearl Harbor to Guadalcanal*, 315.
11. Griffith, *Battle for Guadalcanal*, 135.
12. Hough, *Pearl Harbor to Guadalcanal*, 315.
13. Ibid., 316.
14. Ibid.
15. Evans interview.
16. Ibid.
17. Hoffman, *Chesty*, 165.
18. Ibid.
19. Ibid.
20. Ibid.
21. Ibid.
22. Ibid.
23. Ibid.
24. Ibid.
25. Evans interview.
26. Ibid.
27. Hoffman, *Chesty*, 165.
28. Evans interview.
29. Ibid.
30. Ibid.
31. Ibid.

32. Ibid.

33. Ibid.

34. Ibid.

35. Ibid.

36. Ibid.

37. Hoffman, *Chesty*, 167.

38. Evans interview.

39. Ibid.

40. Ibid.

41. Hoffman, *Chesty*, 167.

42. Ibid.

43. Evans interview.

44. Hoffman, *Chesty*, 167.

Chapter 8. First Family of the Coast Guard

1. Munro family oral history.

2. Ibid.

3. Ibid.

4. Dexter letter.

5. Sheehan interview.

6. Ibid.

7. Munro family papers.

8. Munro family oral history.

9. Ibid.

10. Ibid; Dexter letter.

11. Munro family oral history; Dexter letter.

12. Munro family papers.

13. Munro family oral history.

14. Ibid.

15. Munro family papers.

16. Ibid.

17. Munro family oral history.

18. Ibid.

19. Evans interview.

20. Ibid.

21. Ibid.

22. Munro family papers.

23. Ibid.

24. Munro family oral history.

25. Ibid.

26. Ibid.

27. Brougham, "Morning After."

28. Munro, untitled clipping.

29. Munro family oral history.

30. Douglas A. Munro Medal of Honor Citation.

31. Commission Acceptance.

32. Munro family oral history.

33. Ibid.

34. Thrower-Fairey family papers.

35. Munro family papers.

36. Munro family oral history.

37. Ibid.

38. Ibid.

Chapter 9. Coming Home

1. Coox, "Japan at the End," 2540–2544.

2. Giangreco, *Hell to Pay*, 125–130.

3. Ibid., 45–48.

4. Ibid., 98–99; Frank, *Downfall*, 340.

5. "509 Operations Group."

6. Campbell, *Silverplate Bombers*, 14–15.

7. Ibid., 17.

8. Munro family oral history.

9. Truman, "Statement."

10. Munro family oral history.

11. Truman, "Statement."

12. Munro family oral history.

13. Hoyt, *Japan's War,* 401.

14. "Timeline #3—the 509th."

15. "Imperial Rescript."

16. Munro family oral history.

17. Ibid.

18. Steere and Boardman, *Final Disposition*, 34, 35.

19. Ibid., 35–36.

20. Munro family papers.

21. Munro family oral history.

22. Steere and Boardman, *Final Disposition*, 536.

23. Ibid., 537, 538.

24. Ibid., 538.

25. Ibid.

26. Ibid.

27. Munro family oral history.

28. Ibid.

29. Ibid.

30. Ibid.

31. *Book of Common Prayer.*

32. Munro family oral history.

Chapter 10. Honor, Respect, Devotion to Duty

1. Cooley interview.
2. Ibid.
3. Sheehan interview.
4. Cooley interview.
5. Sheehan interview.
6. Ibid.
7. Ibid.
8. Munro family papers.
9. Munro family oral history.
10. Munro family papers.
11. Ibid.
12. Ibid.
13. Ibid.
14. Sheehan interview.
15. Ibid.
16. Ibid.
17. Munro family papers.
18. Sheehan interview.
19. Ibid.
20. Ibid.
21. Ibid.
22. Craig interview.
23. Ibid.
24. Sheehan interview.
25. Ibid.
26. Patton interview.
27. Ibid.

28. Ibid.

29. Ibid.

30. Ibid.

31. Ibid.

32. Ibid.

33. Ibid.

34. Ibid.

35. Craig interview.

36. Sheehan interview.

37. Patton interview.

38. Ibid.

39. Sheehan interview.

40. Evans interview.

41. Patton interview.

Chapter 11. Coast Guard and Marine Corps Legend

1. Sheehan interview.

Postscript

1. Papp remarks.

BIBLIOGRAPHY

Books, Periodicals, Online Articles, and Miscellaneous Publications

Adams, Michael R. *Ocean Station: Operations of the U.S. Coast Guard, 1940–1977*. Eastport, ME: Nor'easter Press.

Allen, Thomas, and Norman Polmar. *Code-Name Downfall*. New York: Simon & Schuster, 1995.

"Around the Globe." *Coast Guard Magazine* (December 1942): 1–8.

Beau, Jerome J. C. *The U.S. Marine Raiders of WWII: Those Who Served*. Richmond, VA: American Historical Foundation, 1996.

The Book of Common Prayer and Administration of the Sacraments and Other Rites and Ceremonies of the Church According to the Use of the Protestant Episcopal Church in the United States of America. Together with The Psalter or Psalms of David. New York: Church Pension Fund, 1945.

Borleske, Mark. "An Overview of the Milwaukee Road Site South Cle Elum." Cascade Rail Foundation. www.milwelectric.org/history/#overview. Accessed April 8, 2011.

Borneman, Walter R. *The Admirals: Nimitz, Halsey, Leahy and King—the 5-Star Admirals Who Won the War at Sea*. New York: Back Bay Books, 2013.

Brady, James. *Hero of the Pacific: The Life of Marine Legend John Basilone*. Hoboken, NJ: John Wiley & Sons, 2010.

Browning, Robert M. *Douglas Munro at Guadalcanal*. U.S. Coast Guard Historian's Office, n.d.

Campbell, Richard H. *The Silverplate Bombers: A History and Registry of the Enola Gay and Other B-29s Configured to Carry Atomic Bombs*. Jefferson, NC: McFarland, 2005.

Clemens, Martin. *Alone on Guadalcanal: A Coastwatcher's Diary*. Annapolis, MD: Naval Institute Press, 1998.

The Coast Guard at War: The Pacific Landings, VI. Washington, DC: U.S. Coast Guard Historical Division, 1946.

Coox, Alvin D. "Japan at the End of Her Tether." In *History of the Second World War*, vol. 6, by B. H. Liddell Hart. London: Purnell, 2006.

Cressman, Robert J. *The Official Chronology of the U.S. Navy in World War II*. Annapolis, MD: Naval Institute Press, 2000.

Daniels, Jonathan. "1941: Pearl Harbor Sunday: The End of an Era." In *The Aspirin Age: 1919–1941*, edited by Isabel Leighton. New York: Simon & Schuster, 1949.

Douglas Albert Munro: Facts and Comments. Seattle: Coast Guard Museum NW, n.d. Obtained September 26, 2011.

Drea, Edward J. *MacArthur's ULTRA: Codebreaking and the War Against Japan, 1942–1945*. Lawrence: University Press of Kansas, 1992.

Dyer, George C. *The Amphibians Came to Conquer: The Story of Admiral Richmond Kelly Turner*. Washington, DC: Government Printing Office, 1969.

"509 Operations Group (ACC)." Fact Sheet. Air Force Historical Research Agency. http://www.afhra.af.mil.factsheets/factsheet.asp?id=10517. Accessed December 7, 2012.

Frank, Richard B. *Downfall: The End of the Imperial Japanese Empire*. New York: Random House, 1999.

————. *Guadalcanal: The Definitive Account of the Landmark Battle.* New York: Penguin, 1992.

Giangreco, D. M. *Hell to Pay: Operation Downfall and the Invasion of Japan, 1945–1947.* Annapolis, MD: Naval Institute Press, 2009.

The Gold Dust Twins. Washington, DC: U.S. Coast Guard, n.d. Obtained May 5, 2012.

Griffith, Samuel B., II. *The Battle for Guadalcanal.* Annapolis, MD: Nautical & Aviation Publishing, 1963.

Groves, Leslie. *Now It Can Be Told: The Story of the Manhattan Project.* New York: Harper & Row, 1962.

Guadalcanal. The U.S. Army Campaigns of World War II. U.S. Army Center of Military History. http://www.history.army.mil/brochures/72-8/72-8.htm. Accessed September 18, 2011.

Hoffman, Jon T. *Chesty: The Story of Lieutenant General Lewis B. Puller, USMC.* New York: Random House, 2001.

————. *From Makin to Bougainville: Marine Raiders in the Pacific War.* Marines in World War II Commemorative Series. Washington, DC: Marine Corps Historical Center, 1995.

Hornfischer, James D. *Neptune's Inferno: The U.S. Navy at Guadalcanal.* New York: Bantam, 2012.

Hough, Frank O. *Pearl Harbor to Guadalcanal: History of U.S. Marine Corps Operations in World War II.* Washington, DC: Government Printing Office, 1958.

Hoyt, Edwin P. *Japan's War: The Great Pacific Conflict.* New York: Cooper Square Press, 2001.

"Hunter Liggett." DANFS Online. http://www.hazegray.org/danfs/auxil/ap27.htm. Accessed October 4, 2011.

Jersey, Stanley Coleman. *Hell's Islands: The Untold Story of Guadalcanal.* College Station: Texas A&M University Press, 2008.

Johnson, Robert Erwin. *Guardians of the Sea: History of the U.S.C.G., 1915–Present.* Annapolis, MD: Naval Institute Press, 1987.

"Joseph T. Dickman." DANFS Online. http://www.hazegray.org/danfs/auxil/ap26.txt. Accessed October 4, 2011.

Kimball, L. J. "The U.S. Coast Guard at Camp Lejeune, a Brief History." U.S. Coast Guard. www.uscg.mil/history/articles/ CampLejeuneUSCGLJKimball2011.pdf. Accessed July 18, 2014.

The Landing in the Solomons: 7–8 August 1942. U.S. Navy Combat Narrative. Washington, DC: Publications Branch, Office of Naval Intelligence, U.S. Navy, 1943.

Leckie, Robert. *Challenge for the Pacific: The Bloody Six-Month Battle of Guadalcanal.* New York: Da Capo, 1999.

"Leonard Wood." DANFS Online. http://www.hazegray.org/danfs/ amphib/apa12.txt. Accessed October 4, 2011.

Medal of Honor: The Navy, 1861–1949. Washington DC: Bureau of Naval Personnel, 1951.

"Medal of Honor Goes to Mother." *Palm Beach Post,* May 28, 1943.

Miller, Thurman. *Earned in Blood: My Journey from Old-Breed Marine to the Most Dangerous Job in America.* New York: St. Martin's, 2013.

Morison, Samuel Eliot. *The Battle of the Atlantic, September 1939– May 1943.* Vol. 1, *History of United States Naval Operations in World War II.* Boston: Little, Brown, 1947.

———. *The Struggle for Guadalcanal, August 1942–February 1943.* Vol. 5, *History of United States Naval Operations in World War II.* Boston: Little, Brown, 1949.

Newcomb, Richard F. *Savo: The Incredible Naval Debacle Off Guadalcanal.* New York: Holt, Rinehart & Winston, 1961.

Ore, Marion J. *On the Canal: The Marines of L-3-5 on Guadalcanal, 1942.* Mechanicsburg, PA: Stackpole Books, 2004.

Ostrom, Thomas P. *The United States Coast Guard in World War II: A History of Domestic and Overseas Actions.* Jefferson, NC: McFarland, 2009.

"Paul W. Tibbets, Jr, Pilot of Enola Gay, Dies at 92." *New York Times.* www.nytimes.com/2007/11/01/obituaries/01cnd-tibbets.html?pagewanted=all&_r=0.

Potter, E. B., and Chester W. Nimitz. *Sea Power.* New York: Prentice-Hall, 1960.

Quann, C. James. "Douglas A. Munro." *Columbia Magazine* 14, no. 3 (Fall 2000).

Roosevelt, Franklin D. *The Call to Battle Stations: 1941.* Vol 10, *The Public Papers and Addresses of Franklin D. Roosevelt.* New York: Russell & Russell, 1969.

Roscoe, Theodore. *United States Destroyer Operations in World War II.* Annapolis, MD: Naval Institute Press, 1988.

Russ, Martin. *Line of Departure: Tarawa.* Garden City, NY: Doubleday, 1975.

Scheina, Robert. *U.S. Coast Guard Cutters and Craft of World War II.* Annapolis, MD: Naval Institute Press, 1982.

Shaw, Henry I. *First Offensive: The Marine Campaign for Guadalcanal.* Marines in World War II Commemorative Series. Washington, DC: Marine Corps Historical Center, n.d.. Obtained October 16, 2011.

Shideler, John C. *Coal Town in the Cascades: A Centennial History of Roslyn and Cle Elum, Washington.* Spokane: Melior Publications, 1986.

Silverstone, Paul H. *U.S. Warships of World War II.* New York: Doubleday, 1968.

SM1c Douglas A. Munro, USCG. Washington, DC: U.S. Coast Guard, n.d. Obtained May 5, 2012.

"Spencer, 1937." http://www.uscg.mil/history/webcutters/Spencer1937.asp. Accessed October 4, 2011.

Steere, Edward, and Thayer M. Boardman. *Final Disposition of WWII Dead, 1945–1951.* Washington DC: Historical Branch of the Quartermaster General, 1957.

Thomas, Gordon, and Max Morgan-Witts. *Ruin from the Air.* London: Hamilton, 1977.

Thomas, Lowell. *These Men Shall Never Die.* Philadelphia: John C. Winston, 1943.

"Timeline #3—the 509th: The Nagasaki Mission." Atomic Heritage Foundation. http://www.mphpa.org/classic/HISTORY/H-07m1.htm. Accessed December 12, 2013.

Tregaskis, Richard. *Guadalcanal Diary.* New York: Modern Library, 2000.

U.S. Coast Guard: A Historical Overview. Washington, DC: U.S. Coast Guard, n.d.

U.S. Coast Guard, Public Information Division. "The Coast Guard at War: Women's Reserve." Vol. 12. Washington, DC: U.S. Coast Guard, 1946. Obtained August 28, 2013.

U.S. Coast Guard Combat Cutters of World War II. Washington, DC: United States Coast Guard, n.d. Obtained May 5, 2012.

U.S. Coast Guard Cutter History, Spencer, 1937. Washington, DC: U.S. Coast Guard, n.d. Obtained May 5, 2012.

U.S. Coast Guard Historian. "CDR Ray Evans, USCG (Ret.): Transcript of Video Interview Regarding CDR Evans and Douglas Munro." Washington, DC: U.S. Coast Guard, 1999. Obtained May 5, 2012.

Vandegrift, Alexander. *Once a Marine: The Memoirs of General A. A. Vandegrift, U.S.M.C.* New York: W. W. Norton, 1964.

"Wakefield." DANFS Online. http://www.hazegray.org.danfs/auxil/ap21.htm. Accessed October 4, 2011.

Walling, Michael G. *Bloodstained Sea: The U.S. Coast Guard in the Battle of the Atlantic, 1941–1944.* New York: McGraw-Hill, 2004.

White, David Fairbank. *Bitter Ocean: The Battle of the Atlantic, 1939–1945.* New York: Simon & Schuster, 2006.

Willoughby, Malcolm F. *The U.S. Coast Guard in World War II.* Annapolis, MD: United States Naval Institute, 1957.

Interviews

Cooley, Brian. Interview by author, September 26, 2011.
Craig, JoEllen. Interview by author, September 26, 2011.
Eidemiller, James. Interview by author, September 26–27, 2011.
Evans, Ray. Interview by author, September 25–26, 2011.
Jones, Steven. Interview by author, September 26, 2011.

Kayner, Darwin. Interview by author, September 25–26, 2011.

Leavitt, Michael. Interview, May 18, 2012.

Patton, Vince. Interview by author.

Sheehan, Douglas. Interviews by author, September 24–27, 2011; May 17–18, 2012.

Official Documents

Commission Acceptance, Oath of Office. Form NCG9556A, May 27, 1943. In Munro family papers.

"Imperial Rescript Ending War: What Hirohito Really Said in His Acceptance Speech." Translated by William Wetherall. Yosha Research. http://members.jcom.home.ne.jp/yosha/yr/empires/Imperial_rescript_1945-08-14.html. Accessed December 14, 2013.

Munro, Douglas A., Medal of Honor Citation. In Munro family papers.

Truman, Harry S. "Statement by the President Announcing the Use of the A-Bomb at Hiroshima." Public Papers of the Presidents: Harry S. Truman, 1945–1953. Harry S. Truman Library & Museum. http://www.truman library.org/publicpapers/index.php?pid=100&st=Hiroshima&st1=.

Washington State Department of Health: Death certificate, James Munro, April 16, 1962. Received August 26, 2013.

Personal Papers and Private Document Collections

Brougham, Royal. "The Morning After," *Seattle Times*, undated clipping. In Munro family papers.

Collection of Patricia Munro Sheehan.

Dexter, Rear Admiral Dwight H., USCG (Ret.) Letter to the Munro family. In Patricia Munro Sheehan collection.

Hurlbut, James W. Untitled clipping of article published in *Seattle Times*, October 15, 1942. In Munro family papers.

Munro, Edith. Untitled clipping of article published in *Coast Guard Magazine* (April 1943). In Munro family papers.

Munro family papers: Collection of James and Edith Munro. Maintained by Douglas Sheehan.

Papp, Robert, Jr. Remarks at the Dedication of the Douglas A. Munro Coast Guard Headquarters Building, Washington, DC, November 13, 2013.

Personal collection of Bert Caloud.

Personal collection of Darwin Kayner.

Sheehan, Douglas. Remarks on September 27, 2011, Laurel Hill Cemetery, Cle Elum, Washington. Obtained September 27, 2011.

Thrower-Fairey family collection. Maintained by Randall Fairey.

INDEX